THE CONSTITUTIONS OF
THE AUSTRALIAN STATES

The Constitutions
of the
Australian States

R. D. LUMB

Fourth Edition

UNIVERSITY OF QUEENSLAND PRESS

© University of Queensland Press, St. Lucia,
Queensland, 1977
First edition, 1963
Second edition, 1965
Second edition revised 1968
Third edition 1972
Fourth edition

Printed and bound by Silex Enterprise & Printing Co.,
Hong Kong

Distributed in the United Kingdom, Europe, the Middle East,
Africa, and the Caribbean by Prentice-Hall International,
International Book Distributors Ltd., 66 Wood Lane End,
Hemel Hempstead, Herts., England

National Library of Australia
Cataloguing-in-publication data

Lumb, Richard Darrell.
    The constitutions of the Australian states.

    Index.
    ISBN 0 7022 1452 3.

    1. Constitutions, State – Australia. I. Title.

342.9402

Contents

PART I

THE FORMATION OF THE CONSTITUTIONS OF THE AUSTRALIAN STATES

PART II

THE PRESENT STRUCTURE OF THE CONSTITUTIONS OF THE AUSTRALIAN STATES

Preface to the Fourth Edition

In the light of events occurring in the period 1973-1975 which have affected the State Constitutions, it has been necessary to substantially revise certain sections of the book.

A central feature of this period was the tussle between the States and the Commonwealth over the "British connection", i.e., the constitutional ties between the States and the United Kingdom, particularly the continuation of appeals to the Judicial Committee of the Privy Council from State Supreme Courts.

Also during this period the High Court in *New South Wales* v. *Commonwealth* upheld the validity of the Seas and Submerged Lands Act by which the Commonwealth had declared and enacted that sovereignty or sovereign rights in maritime areas adjacent to the Continent of Australia were vested in the Crown in right of the Commonwealth.

Among other events of significance have been the passing of a new Constitution Act in Victoria consolidating and updating the Constitution of that State and amendments to the South Australian Constitution introducing a proportional representation system of voting for elections to the Upper Hoese and entrenching rules relating to electoral re-distribution.

R.D. LUMB

March 1976

Preface to the First Edition

This work was written to fill a gap in the existing literature on Australian constitutional law. It has been written primarily for students and as such attempts to place in a general perspective those features of the State Constitutions which are considered to be of most importance.

I wish to thank Professor W.N.L. Harrison, Garrick Professor of Law, and Professor E.I. Sykes, Professor of Public Law, in the University of Queensland, for reading the manuscript with critical eyes. My thanks are also due to Misses J. Droughton, M. Emmett, and M. Ham for typing the manuscript. I wish to acknowledge the original stimulus to thought on the subject provided by Professor R. Anderson, late Professor of Public Law in the University of Queensland.

R.D. LUMB
University of Queensland
St. Lucia

November 1962

Preface to the Second Edition

In the second edition of this work I have taken account of a number of comments and suggestions made by reviewers and have enlarged certain sections (e.g. extraterritorial legislative power) in the light of recent decisions and discussions in the journals. A number of appendices have been added.

R.D. LUMB
University of Queensland
St. Lucia

April 1965

Preface to the Third Edition

I have taken the opportunity in this, the third edition of the work, to update the text and footnote references in the light of statutory changes and recent judicial decisions. References to recent articles in the periodicals have also been incorporated.

R.D. LUMB

May 1971

Table of Important Statutes
(*in chronological order*)

Table of Cases

Introduction

THE CONSTITUTIONAL FRAMEWORK OF AUSTRALIA is associated more often than not with the federal structure brought into existence by the Commonwealth of Australia Constitution Act of 1900 and the interpretations of that Act by the courts. However, it must be pointed out that the Commonwealth Constitution Act, while it had the effect of federating the colonies of the Australian continent and of raising them to the dignity of States of the Commonwealth, did not replace the pre-existing Constitutions of the States. In fact s. 106 of the Constitution provides that, subject to the Commonwealth Constitution, the Constitutions of each State shall continue in force at the establishment of the Commonwealth. The federal nature of the Australian constitutional structure was re-affirmed by the High Court in the Airlines Case[1] and the words of Kitto, J., may be called to mind: "The Australian union is one of dual federalism and until the Parliament and the people see fit to change it, a true federation it must remain."[2]

In contrast with the Commonwealth Constitution, which can only be altered by a complex procedure, most provisions of the Constitutions of the States can be altered by legislation passed in the ordinary manner. This accounts for the numerous changes which have been made to such Constitutions both during this century and the nineteenth century in response to the changing demands and needs of the various State communities. Consequently the State Constitutions, while exhibiting certain uniform features, differ in significant respects. It is necessary therefore to have some knowledge of the historical setting in which they were developed in order to understand their present structure.

In this work it will be my task to examine the salient features of the Constitutions of the States. This will involve not only a study of the relevant statutes and legal decisions but also of the conventions they presuppose. In the first part of this work I will examine the historical steps which led to the grant of responsible government to each of the colonies, while in the second part the present structure of the Constitutions will be analysed.

[1] *Airlines of New South Wales Pty. Ltd.* v. *The State of New South Wales* (No. 2) (1964-65) 113 C.L.R. 54.
[2] *Ibid.*, at p. 115.

PART I

The Formation of the Constitutions of the Australian States

CHAPTER ONE

New South Wales

TODAY THE CONSTITUTIONS of the States of Australia are characterized by the features of representative and responsible government. It is important to keep in mind that these features were the product of gradual evolution and did not accompany the establishment of legislative authority in the infant colonies of Australia.[1] Dr. Jenks has succinctly stated the course of development which a settled colony has usually undergone:

> First there has been a purely despotic government, when the colony has been ruled as a military position by a Governor and a handful of officials appointed by the Home Government. Then there has been a constitution, with a Legislative Council, partly appointed by the Government and partly elective. Of the Council the Crown officials have always formed part, but the executive has been unassailable by the legislature and responsible only to the Colonial Office; possessions in these two stages being known technically as Crown Colonies. In the third stage, there have generally been two Houses of the legislature, both elective, or one elective and one nominee, and the executive has consisted of officials chosen for their Parliamentary position and liable to be dismissed, like ministers in England, in consequence of an adverse vote of the legislature. This is the era of Responsible Government.[2]

The fact that New South Wales was a place to which convicts were transported contributed to the slowness in the development of independent legal institutions representing the inhabitants of the country. Indeed, as a number of writers have pointed out, it is doubtful whether, in the years that followed the first landing, New South Wales had the

---

[1] For a comprehensive analysis of the development of the Constitution of New South Wales, see J. Quick and R. R. Garran, *The Annotated Constitution of the Australian Commonwealth* (Sydney: Angus & Robertson, 1901), pp. 35-51; A.C.V. Melbourne, *Early Constitutional Development in Australia: New South Wales 1788-1856, Queensland 1859-1922*, ed. R. B. Joyce (2nd ed.; St. Lucia: University of Queensland Press, 1963); also E. Sweetman, *Australian Constitutional Development* (Melbourne: Macmillan & Co. and Melbourne University Press, 1925).

It is necessary to point out that the word "Constitution" is used in the present work in a general sense to refer to the the body of principles governing the legal framework of the colonies irrespective of whether such principles are to be found in a single Constitution Act or not.

[2] E. Jenks, *The Government of Victoria* (London: Macmillan & Co., 1891), p.11.

status of an ordinary colony. In so far as a military government was established in the territory, the majority of its subjects being under penal discipline, and the applicability of English law remaining uncertain, these writers have preferred to regard New South Wales as a penal settlement.[3]

The circumstances surrounding the foundation of New South Wales are as follows.

In 1770 Captain Cook had taken possession of the eastern coast of Australia on behalf of the Crown. With the loss of the American colonies, it was necessary for the British authorities to find new overseas places to which to send convicts. An Imperial Act of 1784, 24 Geo. III, c.56, had given the King-in-Council power to declare places in or out of the dominion as places to which convicts might be transported: New South Wales was declared such a place by Orders in Council made in 1786.[4] In that year also a Commission was issued to Phillip appointing him Governor of New South Wales. This was followed by another Commission in 1787.[5] An Act of the Imperial Parliament of 1787, 27 Geo. III, c.2, provided that the person occupying the position of Governor should have authority from time to time to convene a Court of Criminal Judicature with authority to try offences which, if committed in England, would constitute treason, felony, or misdemeanour.[6] No direct authority to establish a civil government was created by the Act although in the recitals reference was made to the fact that it might be found necessary in the future to establish such a government. However, subsequent to the Act, letters patent (later known as the First Charter of Justice) were issued establishing courts of both criminal and civil jurisdiction. The civil jurisdiction covered pleas concerning land, pleas for debt, account and other contracts, and certain other pleas. The criminal jurisdiction clauses provided for punishment according to the laws of England taking into account the circumstances of the colony and its inhabitants.[7]

There has been much speculation as to the constitutional validity of

---

[3] See T. P. Webb, *A Compendium of Imperial Law and Statutes in Force in Victoria* (2nd ed.; Melbourne: Robertson & Mullens, 1892), pp. 9 *et seq.*; Jenks, *The Government of Victoria*, p.11; H. V. Evatt, "The Legal Foundations of New South Wales", 11 *Australian Law Journal* (1938), 409.

[4] See Melbourne, *Early Constitutional Development in Australia*, chap. 1.

[5] See W. J. V. Windeyer, "A Birthright and Inheritance: the Establishment of the Rule of Law in Australia", 1 *Tasmanian University Law Review* (1962), 635. As Sir Victor points out, the first commission was a military one, and the second a civil one.

[6] Evatt, "The Legal Foundations of New South Wales", p. 412.

[7] *Ibid.*

the orders of the Governor regulating the affairs of New South Wales and of the steps taken to establish and exercise civil jurisdiction. It is said that the only valid exercise of authority over a colony could be derived from the Imperial Parliament or from a local assembly: according to this view the exercise of legislative power by the Crown or its delegate, the Governor, infringed a fundamental principle of constitutional practice. Webb, following Bentham, has expressed the opinion that the Act of 1787 lacked the essential features on the basis of which one might attribute to New South Wales the status of a settled colony, that the settlement was merely a penal one, and that it was not until 1823 when a civil government was established that New South Wales became a colony. In his view the erection of a court of civil jurisdiction was unconstitutional.[8] Evatt, however, considers that although New South Wales was not a full colony, the establishment by letters patent of a court of civil jurisdiction meant that the court was to apply English law so far as it was applicable to the circumstances of the colony. Such law could be supplemented by orders and regulations of the Governor even though no express power was conferred on him by the 1787 Act to legislate for the colony.[9] Evatt's view is then that, despite the absence of Imperial legislation providing for the application of English law, New South Wales was a colony (albeit of a penal nature) in which both English civil and criminal law so far as it was applicable operated.

More recently, Windeyer, Else-Mitchell, and Campbell have examined the legal issues pertaining to the foundation of New South Wales and have come to the conclusion that the regulations or orders made by the Governors were, subject to certain qualifications, valid, and that the establishment of civil jurisdiction in the colony was not unconstitutional. As Windeyer puts it, "the colony was under a form of military administration certainly; but it was a military administration of civil affairs, to use modern terms".[10] R. E. Else-Mitchell, however, enters the caveat that certain of the Governor's orders, in particular those imposing taxes, could not be justified under any of the

---

[8] Webb, *A Compendium of Imperial Law and Statutes in Force in Victoria*, p. 23; J. Bentham, "A Plea for the Constitution of New South Wales", *Life and Works*, ed. J. Bowring (Edinburgh: W. Tait, 1843), IV, 254, *et seq*. See also W. B. Campbell, "A Note on Jeremy Bentham's 'A Plea for the Constitution of New South Wales' ", 25 *Australian Law Journal* (1951), 59.

[9] Evatt, "The Legal Foundations of New South Wales", pp. 420-21.

[10] Windeyer, "A Birthright and Inheritance: the Establishment of the Rule of Law in Australia", p. 643.

powers conferred on the first Governors by their Commissions.[11] Enid Campbell expresses doubts as to whether the principle prohibiting legislation by prerogative act applied to a colony such as New South Wales although she too considers that taxes could not be imposed by gubernatorial order.[12] All these writers agree that the establishment of the court of civil jurisdiction by prerogative act was not contrary to constitutional practice.[13]

It seems that the view expressed by Evatt and these later writers (although differing among themselves in some points of detail) is closer to the reality of the situation than that expressed by the critics of prerogative rule. In the first place, the peculiar circumstances of New South Wales already referred to demanded that the power of regulating the affairs of the colony be vested in the representative of the Crown until a local legislature could be set up, subject to the limitation that "important" matters could only be dealt with by the Imperial Parliament; and it is clear that the royal prerogative also provided an ample basis for the erection of the court of civil jurisdiction. In the second place the laws of England which were applicable to the circumstances of New South Wales were in force in the colony.[14] In the words of Counsel to the Board of Plantations in an opinion given in 1740:

> The common law of England is the common law of the plantations and all statutes in affirmance of the common law passed in England, antecedent to the settlement of the colony, are in force in that colony, unless there is some private Act to the contrary ... Let an Englishman go where he will, he carries as much of the law and liberty with him as the nature of things will bear.[15]

This general principle was applied to New South Wales by the Privy

---

[11]"The Foundation of New South Wales and the Inheritance of the Common Law", 49 *Royal Australian Historical Society Journal* (1963), 5.
[12]"Prerogative Rule in New South Wales 1788-1823", 50 *Royal Australian Historical Society Journal* (1964), 181 *et seq.*
[13]Windeyer, "A Birthright and Inheritance: the Establishment of the Rule of Law in Australia", p. 649; Else-Mitchell, "The Foundation of New South Wales and the Inheritance of the Common Law", p. 4; Enid Campbell, "The Royal Prerogative to Create Colonial Courts", 4 *Sydney Law Review* (1964), 343.
[14]See W. J. V. Windeyer, *Lectures on Legal History* (2nd ed.; Sydney: Law Book Co. of Australasia, 1957), p. 304.
[15]W. Forsyth, *Cases and Opinions on Constitutional Law* (London: Stevens & Haynes, 1869), p. 21. A recent application of this principle is the decision of Blackburn, J., of the Northern Territory Supreme Court, that on settlement rights to land in the colony vested in the Crown and consequently the aborigines had no communal legal title in such lands: *Milirrpum and ors. v. Nabalco Pty. Ltd. and the Commonwealth of Australia* (1971) 17 F.L.R. 141.

Council in *Cooper* v. *Stuart*[16] where it was said:

The extent to which English law is introduced into a British colony, and the manner of the introduction, must necessarily vary according to the circumstances. There is a great difference between the case of a colony acquired by conquest or cession, in which there is an established system of law, and that of a colony which consisted of a tract or territory practically unoccupied with settled inhabitants, or settled law, at the time when it was peacefully annexed to the British dominion. The colony of New South Wales belongs to the latter class. In the case of such a colony the Crown may by ordinance, and the Imperial Parliament, or its own legislature, when it comes to possess one, may by statute declare what parts of the common and statute law of England shall have effect within its limits. But when that is not done, the law of England must (subject to well-established exceptions) become from the outset the law of the colony, and be administered by its tribunals. In so far as it is reasonably applicable to the circumstances of the colony, the law of England must prevail until it is abrogated or modified either by ordinance or statute.[17]

The position in the formative years of New South Wales may then be stated as follows. Although New South Wales was a penal colony, the statute law and common law of England were in force from 1788 so far as they were applicable to the local circumstances (i.e. taking into account the penal nature of the colony). Supreme legal authority over the area was vested in the Imperial Parliament. In the absence of Imperial legislation setting out the powers of the Governor, the right of making ordinances and regulations was vested in the Crown or its representative in the colony, the Governor (acting under a Commission issued by the Crown), such ordinances and regulations to be consistent with the laws of England so far as applicable. This last phrase is of crucial importance. The early Governors of New South Wales in fact exercised their powers of supplementing English law and in some cases modified it, for example, with respect to matters of public order. In view of the circumstances of the colony, such modification could not be regarded as unconstitutional or illegal.[18] The Governor himself was subject to directions from the Home Government through the Secretary of State for the Colonies but with the infrequency of com-

---

[16](1889) 14 App. Cas. 286.
[17]*Ibid.*, p. 291. See, however, Enid Campbell, "Prerogative Rule in New South Wales 1788-1823", pp. 186-87, who is inclined to question the authority of this dictum.
[18]Windeyer, *Lectures on Legal History*, pp. 305-6.

munications between the two countries he had a wide discretion in the administration of the affairs of the colony.[19]

Between the years 1788 and 1823 the personal rule of the Governor continued in the absence of Imperial legislation establishing a local legislature. This rule however was not without constitutional crises. On one occasion the validity of an ordinance was called into question on the ground that there was a conflict between it and the law of England, but the Secretary of State upheld the Governor.[20] There was in this period no precise legal evaluation of what principles of English law were paramount nor to what extent they could be modified in the light of the local circumstances of New South Wales. At least it could be said that trial by jury was one principle which was not considered as appropriate to these circumstances.[21] With the establishment of a Supreme Court by letters patent in 1814 (the Second Charter of Justice) judicial review of the Governor's orders became more feasible and the following statement by the Judge of the Supreme Court (J. H. Bent) exemplifies the increasing hostility of the judges to some of the Governor's actions:

I am required to admit that to be legal and founded on sure authority which I know to be otherwise, and to acknowledge that your Excellency's will, expressed by proclamation, by what is termed a government order, or a government notice, has the force and validity of law, a proposition so startling that I cannot conceive any person in England, much less any lawyer, could have the slightest notion that it would be maintained even in argument, far otherwise that it would be attempted to be carried out in its fullest extent in practice.

The attitude of the Secretary of State to the issue was expressed in a reply to earlier correspondence from the Judge's brother Ellis Bent, the Deputy Judge-Advocate, who had adopted a similar view of the legality of the orders.

I have only to observe that the power of the Governor to issue government and general orders, in the absence of all other authority, and the necessity of obeying them, rests now on the same foundation on which it ever stood since the first formation of the colony ... [22]

---

[19] K.R. Cramp, *State and Federal Constitutions of Australia* (2nd ed.; Sydney: Angus & Robertson, 1914), p. 8.

[20] Melbourne, *Early Constitutional Development in Australia*, p. 33. The Governor at this time was Macquarie.

[21] Trial by jury was not finally established in criminal cases till 1839. See Windeyer, *Lectures on Legal History*, p. 312.

[22] Melbourne, *Early Constitutional Development in Australia*, p. 33. Enid

The doubts of the judiciary however were not quieted and the imposition of taxes on the importation of spirits and tobacco gave rise to discussion of the question which had been at the root of the conflict between England and the American colonies—taxation of the inhabitants of a colony otherwise than by a representative legislature. The Secretary of State sought the advice of Counsel. The answer received was that laws for the levying of taxes could not be made by virtue of the royal prerogative but only by Act of Parliament. Subsequently the Imperial Parliament passed retrospective legislation to validate the exaction of taxes and to provide for the continuation of existing duties.[23]

A further dispute as to the validity of the Governor's ordinances occurred when the Governor's Court (a court of superior jurisdiction established in 1814) held that a proclamation issued by the Governor in 1818 with respect to the conferment of jurisdiction on Magistrates' Courts was invalid. Here again the Secretary of State, to whom the matter had been referred, sought the opinion of Counsel. In this opinion, a distinction was made between colonies acquired by conquest or cession on the one hand and colonies acquired by occupation on the other hand.[24] In the latter case the law of England in so far as it was applicable was in force but

> the invariable usage in all such cases has been to require the Governor to convene an Assembly elected by the freeholders within the colony; and thus the colonists have lived under the constitution of England, varied only so as to meet the new circumstances in which they have been placed; and that for His Majesty to confer a legislative power on the Governor alone, and without the control of a local Assembly, would be to deprive the colonists of the constitution and laws which, it is admitted, they are to carry with them.[25]

The general effect of this opinion was to deny in general the right of the Governor to enact laws without the advice of a representative as-

Campbell, in her article, "Prerogative Rule in New South Wales", p. 174, is of the opinion that judicial opposition was based on the ground that the orders were repugnant to the laws of England.

[23] Melbourne, *Early Constitutional Development in Australia*, pp. 34-35.

[24] Following W. Blackstone, *Commentaries on the Laws of England* (London: John Murray, 1857), I, 90.

[25] *Historical Records of Australia*, IV, i, 414. See also Forsyth, *Cases and Opinions on Constitutional Law*, p. 20, where there is a statement to the effect that in the case of colonies established by occupancy and settlement, the Crown alone cannot legislate but it may by virtue of its prerogative appoint governors and erect courts of justice and confer the power of summoning representative legislatures. Cf. *Campbell v. Hall* (1774) 1 Cowp. 204, considered in *Sabally v. H. M. Attorney-General* [1964] 3 W.L.R. 732.

sembly.[26] However, even if we regard the requirement of a representative assembly as of a legal and not merely of a political nature, New South Wales because of its penal origin was not in the same position as an ordinary colony and consequently the usage referred to could not be regarded as applicable to the circumstances of the colony—at least in 1818. However, these circumstances were slowly changing with the increase in the number of free citizens who were becoming more vocal in their demands for a local legislature. The Home Government subsequently appointed Commissioner Bigge to enquire into the state of the colony and to suggest reforms which might be necessary. Bigge's recommendations were incorporated in the Act of 1823[27] under which New South Wales attained the status of a full colony.

The provisions of this Act which have the most important constitutional significance are ss. 24 and 29. The recitals to s. 24 referred to the need for a body to make laws and ordinances for the welfare and good government of the colony of New South Wales and to the fact that it was not expedient at that time to summon a Legislative Assembly (a representative body). The section constituted a Legislative Council consisting of residents of the colony (not less than five nor more than seven) to be appointed by the Crown. It vested in the Governor acting with the advice of the Council (or a major part of the Council) power to make laws and ordinances for the peace, welfare and good government of the colony. It provided that such laws and ordinances were not be repugnant to the Act, or the charters, letters patent or Orders in Council to be issued in pursuance thereof, or to the laws of England, "but to be consistent with such laws so far as the circumstances of the said colony will admit". The Governor was given the sole right to lay bills before the Council. A bill was not to become law if all or the majority of the members of the Council dissented from it, except in cases where the Governor was convinced that a proposed law or ordinance was essential to the pace and safety of the colony and would cause extreme injury to the colony if rejected. In such cases the assent of at least one member was a sufficient prerequisite to its validity.[28] Other sections of the Act provided that in the case of rebellion or insurrection, or apprehended rebellion or insurrection, the

---

[26] Such an assembly was not to come into existence in New South Wales for many years.
[27] Geo. IV, C.96. The recommendations of Bigge are examined in Melbourne, *Early Constitutional Development in Australia*, pp. 74-87.
[28] S. 24.

Governor was vested with absolute authority to enforce any law,[29] no tax was to be levied except for local purposes,[30] while the Crown by Order in Council could pass any law which had been dissented from by the whole or major part of the Legislative Council.[31]

Section 29 introduced a form of judicial review of proposed legislation. It prescribed that no law or ordinance was to be laid before the Council until a copy had been laid before the Chief Justice of the Supreme Court. It was the duty of the Chief Justice to certify to the Governor that the proposed law was not repugnant to the laws of England but was consistent with them so far as the circumstances of the colony would admit. Further sections imposed additional controls over the local authorities by vesting in the Crown power to disallow within three years any ordinance or law[32] and requiring all laws and ordinances to be laid before the Imperial Parliament.[33] Pursuant to the 1823 Act, letters patent (the Third Charter of Justice) were issued establishing a new Supreme Court of which Sir Francis Forbes was appointed Chief Justice.

It can be seen then that the powers of self-government conferred by the 1823 Act were meagre. The Governor (who was also the chief executive officer) together with a Council of members appointed by the Crown constituted the legislature but the Governor also had the sole right of initiating proposed legislation. In normal circumstances a proposed bill would only be enacted into law with the assent of a majority of members, in the case of extreme need by the Governor with the assent of one member only, and in the case of public emergency by the Governor alone. However, the laws made were required to be in conformity with the law of England so far as it was applicable and provision was made for judicial review on this ground. Some protection for the local inhabitants in the matter of taxes was given by that section which prescribed that taxes could only be levied for local needs. However, the overall supervision of the Home Government and the Imperial Parliament was ensured by the provisions relating to disallowance and laying before the Imperial Parliament. The 1823 Act was, however, only meant to be temporary. It was provided that it should continue in force until the end of the next session of Parliament

[29] S. 25.
[30] S. 27.
[31] S. 26.
[32] S. 30.
[33] S. 31.

after 1827.[34]

One important development after the coming into force of the 1823 Act was the creation of an Executive Council pursuant to a new Commission and Instructions issued to the Governor in 1825. The Instructions named certain officials of the colony as members of the Executive Council and the Governor was directed in all things to consult the Council and to act on its advice except when it was necessary to make decisions of an urgent nature or when the interests of the Crown would be adversely affected by consultation. However, the Governor was given power to act contrary to the opinion of the Council, although in such cases he was to inform the Secretary of State of the reasons for his action.[35] The creation of this body can be regarded as a turning point in the autocratic rule of the Governors.

Between 1823 and 1828 the temporary constitution was subject to discussion and suggestions were made, *inter alia*, for the enlargement of the legislative chamber as a representative body and for the modification of the pre-enactment supervisory powers of the Chief Justice over proposed legislation.[36] When the period provided for in the 1823 Act expired, the Imperial Parliament in 1828 passed a new act.[37] This act introduced reforms along the above lines without however making provision for a representative legislature. The size of the Legislative Council was increased by giving the Crown power to nominate not more than fifteen nor less than ten members.[38] The Governor and Legislative Council were given power to legislate for the peace, order, and good government of the colony, such laws to be consistent with the laws of England so far as circumstances would allow.[39] The Governor was deprived of the powers which he had under the 1823 Act of legislating in extreme need with the advice of only one member of the Council and of legislating alone in cases of insurrec-

---

[34] S. 45.

[35] Melbourne, *Early Constitutional Development in Australia*, pp. 108-9.

[36] *Ibid.*, pp. 140-51.

[37] 9 Geo. IV., C.83, later known as the Australian Courts Act. The Bill was drafted by Forbes and was with certain amendments adopted by the Imperial authorities. It has been described by Else-Mitchell, "The Foundation of New South Wales and the Inheritance of the Common Law", p. 20, as marking the establishment of the rule of law on the Australian continent.

[38] S. 20. The Crown followed the practice of appointing an equal number of official and non-official members. See Melbourne, *Early Constitutional Development in Australia*, p. 171.

[39] S. 21. For a detailed study of the effect of the laws of England on the local legislation of the colony see Enid Campbell, "Colonial Legislation and the Laws of England", 2 *Tasmanian University Law Review* (1965), 148 at 155 *et seq.*

tion.[40] Furthermore, in contrast to the 1823 Act, the dissent of a majority of the members of the Council was a bar to the enactment of a proposed bill.[41] The supervisory power of the Chief Justice was modified in the following way. Within seven days of enactment, every law or ordinance was to be enrolled in the Supreme Court. If before the expiration of fourteen days the Judges of the Supreme Court declared that the law or ordinance was repugnant to the Act or to the laws of England, the Governor was to suspend the operation of the law and resubmit it to the Legislative Council. If the Governor and Council continued to adhere to the law it was to have force until the pleasure of the Crown was known.[42] On the qestion of applicability of English law, it was provided that the laws of England (common law and statute law) in force in England at the time of the Act (i.e. 1828) so far as they were applicable were to be in force in New South Wales. Pending a decision by the Governor and Legislative Council as to what laws were applicable, the Supreme Court was to decide the matter when it was in issue in proceedings before that Court.[43] The overall supervision of the Crown was retained in the provision that it might disallow a colonial law within four years from its enactment although the Crown had no power, as it had under the 1823 Act, to enact for New South Wales legislation which had been dissented from by the Legislative Council.[44] The provision for laying legislation before both Houses of the Imperial Parliament was continued in force.[45]

The 1828 Act was also regarded as a temporary measure and kept in operation by successive enactments.[46] Although no provision was

[40] Powers which of course had detracted from the authority conferred on the old Council.
[41] S. 21.
[42] S. 22.
[43] S. 24. The exact phraseology was that all laws and statutes in force within England at the time of the passing of the Act "shall be applied in the administration of justice in the Courts of New South Wales and Van Diemen's Land so far as the same can be applied within the said Colonies". It must be noted that the Governor and Legislative Council did not have merely a declaratory function: they could amend and modify English law which was applicable to the circumstances of the colony in 1828. However, see Enid Campbell, "Colonial Legislation and the Laws of England", pp.166-67. See also *Quan Yick* v. *Hinds* (1904-5) 2 C.L.R. 345; *Delohery* v. *Permanent Trustee Co. of New South Wales* (1903-4) 1 C.L.R. 283; *Mitchell* v. *Scales* (1907) 5 C.L.R. 405; Windeyer, "A Birthright and Inheritance: the Establishment of the Rule of Law in Australia", pp.667-69; and A. C. Castles, "The Reception and Status of English Law in Australia", 2 *Adelaide Law Review* (1963), 1.
[44] S. 28.
[45] S. 29.
[46] Sweetman, *Australian Constitutional Development*, p.74. The 1839 Act (2 & 3 Vict., c.70) contained a new provision which gave to the local legislature power to regulate the judicial structure of the colony. See Melbourne, *Early Constitutional*

made for elected members in the legislature it was recognized that when the colony was ready for some form of representative government the Imperial Parliament would legislate in that respect.[47] It was not until 1842 that provision was made for this form of government. In that year the Imperial Parliament passed "an Act for the Government of New South Wales and Van Diemen's Land".[48] This Act, known as the Australian Constitutions Act (No. 1), established a Legislative Council to consist of thirty-six members of whom two-thirds were to be elected and only one-third appointed by the Crown.[49] The appointment of the non-elective members might be delegated to the Governor in which case the appointments were to be subject to the royal assent.[50] The Governor and Council were given power to increase the number of members of the Legislative Council subject to the condition that the proportion of elected to nominated members (two to one) should remain the same.[51] The qualifications of electors were ownership of a freehold estate of £200 or occupancy of a dwelling-house of a clear annual value of £20.[52]

Legislative power was conferred on the Governor with the advice and consent of the Legislative Council to make laws for the peace, welfare, and good government of the colony. This authority was subject to the previously existing condition that laws which were passed should not be repugnant to the laws of England and a new condition that they should not interfere with the sale or appropriation of Crown lands within the colony or the revenue arising therefrom.[53]

The Governor, although not a member of the legislature as under the old system, was given power to transmit to the Council any bill for

---

Development in Australia, p.198. The 1840 Act, 3 & 4 Vict., c.62, while continuing in operation for a further period the 1828 Act, also made provision for the erection of new colonies. By letters patent of the same year the territory of New Zealand was separated from New South Wales and erected into a separate colony.

[47] As Sweetman points out the continuance of transportation until 1840 was the main reason why the Home Government delayed the introduction of representative government. Sweetman, *Australian Constitutional Development*, pp.74-75.

[48] 5 & 6 Vict., c.76. In actual fact the Act applied in New South Wales only and in a later Act, 7 & 8 Vict., c.74, s.6, it was provided that the reference to New South Wales and Van Diemen's Land was to be taken as a reference to New South Wales only.

[49] S. 1. Both elected and nominated members were to hold office for five years. A person could not be elected unless he held freehold worth £2,000 or of an annual value of £100: s.8.

[50] S. 12.

[51] S. 4.

[52] S. 5.

[53] S. 29.

the consideration of the Council.[54] Any bill which had been passed by
the Council was to be presented for the royal assent to the Governor
who was enjoined to exercise his discretion of assenting to or withholding his assent from a bill according to the terms of the Act or to
instructions which he had received from the Crown. Certain classes of
bills (including bills imposing custom duties) were to be reserved for
the royal assent.[55] Any bills assented to by the Governor might be an-
nulled by the Crown within two years.[56]

The power of the Legislative Council to control the revenue of the
colony was subject to limitations. The Act made the revenue derived
from taxes, rates, and duties on inhabitants within the colony subject
to legislative appropriation but only after a recommendation had been
made by the Governor.[57] Other revenue (such as that derived from
fines and penalties and from Crown land) was not subject to legislative
appropriation.[58] The Act also made provision for the allocation of a
certain yearly sum for the purposes of a Civil List and for public
worship.[59] Provision was also made for the creation of a system of
District Councils with local government powers.[60] Finally, the provisions of the 1828 Act in so far as they had not been amended were
made permanent.[61]

It can be seen that, while the Australian Constitutions Act (No. 1)
made provision for legislative authority to be vested in a body the majority of members of which would be elected by the local inhabitants, it
did not prescribe that the executive should be responsible to the
legislature, and the strict limitation of the legislature's financial powers
left the Governor in control of the "power of the purse".[62] Moreover,
assent to legislation of the Council was within the discretion of the
Governor who was responsible to the Home Government and not to
the Council.

Another important feature of the Act was the omission of the re-

---

[54] S. 30.
[55] S. 31. The bills declared by this section to require reservation were bills altering
electoral divisions, altering the mode of representation in the Council, affecting the
salaries of certain public officials, and affecting customs duties.
[56] S. 32.
[57] S. 34.
[58] See Melbourne, *Early Constitutional Development in Australia*, p.271. These
were known as the casual revenues of the Crown.
[59] S. 37. The Civil List contains the appropriations of public moneys for the salaries
and pensions of public officers.
[60] S. 41.
[61] S. 53.
[62] Melbourne, *Early Constitutional Development in Australia*, p.272.

quirement that the bill be enrolled in the Supreme Court after enactment and be subject to review by the judges. However, this did not mean that the New South Wales courts were deprived of their judicial power of invalidating local legislation on the ground of repugnancy —they had the power to do so whenever a question of the validity of a statute arose in the course of ordinary proceedings.

The Act was proclaimed in the colony in 1843 and the first elections were held in that year. In the ensuing years further efforts were made by the inhabitants of the colony to secure responsible government, resentment being directed against those provisions of the 1842 Act which secured executive independence from the legislature by the provision of a Civil List in the Act and by the omission of certain revenues from legislative appropriation.[63] In 1846 a bill was passed by the Legislative Council declaring officials whose salaries were provided for in the 1842 Act or who otherwise held an office of profit to be disqualified from being elected to the Council. This move was designed to weaken the influence of the Governor in the deliberations of the Chamber. The bill was reserved and did not receive the royal assent.[64] The Council also lost no opportunity in embarrassing the Governor in respect of the financial administration of the colony. A bill was passed by the Council providing for the auditing of the accounts of the ordinary revenue of the colony, the intention being that this would give the legislature some supervisory power over financial administration. However, royal assent was not given to this bill.[65] At the same time, other moves to reform the constitution were in progress. Residents of the Port Phillip district of the colony (which had been placed under the administration of a Superintendent in 1840) were advocating the formation of a separate government for the district, basing their argument on its rapid development.[66] In 1849 a committee of the Privy Council was set up to enquire into the constitutional position of the Australian colonies and its report was the

---

[63] *Ibid.*, pp. 308-16. Under the Waste Lands Act of 1842 (5 & 6 Vict., c.36) the sale of Crown lands and the disposition of the proceeds thereof were made subject to certain conditions and procedures. This had the effect of putting the Governor in a position of "comparative independence". See Melbourne, *Early Constitutional Development in Australia*, at p.273. See also Enid Campbell, "Crown Land Grants: Form and Validity", 40 *Australian Law Journal* (1966), 35.

[64] *Ibid.*, pp.284-85.

[65] *Ibid.*, pp.312-13. However, the Home Government ultimately decided to meet the colony's demand that the casual revenues should be made available for legislative appropriation. *Ibid.*, pp.315-16.

[66] *Ibid.*, pp.331-46.

basis of the Australian Constitutions Act (No. 2) passed in 1850.[67]

This Act did not fulfil the expectations of those who clamoured for reform because it did not modify the relationship between the legislature and the executive, it continued the system of fixed appropriations[68] for the civil service, and continued to exclude the land revenue from legislative appropriation.[69] On the credit side, it separated the Port Philip district from New South Wales and gave to that district a separate legislative council (the proportion of elected to non-elected members being the same as in New South Wales [two to one]),[70] and empowered the existing legislatures of South Australia and Van Diemen's Land to admit elected members to their legislatures in the same proportion.[71] Provision was made for the establishment of a similar legislature in Western Australia on the fulfilment of certain conditions.[72] The Act also empowered the Legislative Councils of New South Wales, Victoria (Port Phillip), Van Diemen's Land, South Australia, and Western Australia (after the establishment of legislative councils as provided for the Act) to alter the constitution of the legislatures and to establish bicameral legislatures in place of the single chambers. However, bills altering the constitutions in this manner were to be reserved for the royal assent.[73] The qualifications of electors for the New South Wales Council were liberalized with the reduction of the property qualifications to £100 for a freehold estate and £10 for the occupancy of a dwelling-house.[74] These qualifications were to be applicable to the Councils of the other colonies when established according to the provisions of the Act.[75]

The Governor and Council were to have power to make laws for the peace, welfare, and good government of the respective colonies subject to certain limitations.[76] Administration of Crown lands was outside

---

[67]"An Act for the better Government of Her Majesty's Australian Colonies", 13 & 14 Vict., c.59. The Report is set out in E. S. Blackmore, *The South Australian Constitution* (Adelaide: Government Printer, 1894), pp.153-58. See also J. M. Ward, *Early Grey and the Australian Colonies*, 1846-57 (Melbourne: Melbourne University Press, 1958), for a discussion of the historical background.

[68]S. 17. However, by S. 18 power was given to the local legislatures to alter the appropriation of such sums. Bills affecting certain appropriations were to be reserved for the royal assent.

[69]S. 14.

[70]Ss. 1, 2.

[71]S. 7.

[72]S. 9.

[73]S. 32.

[74]S. 4.

[75]S. 12.

[76]S. 14.

their province[77] and appropriation bills were to be first recommended by the Governor.[78] Funds for the Civil Lists were laid down in schedules attached to the Act although the amounts could in general be varied by the legislatures (subject to the requirement of reservation in certain cases).[79] Customs duties, provided that they did not fall within certain classes, could be imposed by the local legislature.[80] Finally, provision was made for the separation of the northern part of New South Wales (northward of the thirtieth degree of south latitude)[81] and for the establishment of a legislative council therein by Imperial Order in Council upon the petition of the inhabitants of that area.[82]

It was quite clear in the discussion that followed the enactment of the Australian Constitutions Act (No. 2) that the inhabitants of New South Wales were not satisfied with the concessions that were made. In particular the withholding of responsible government and legislative power over Crown lands (from which considerable revenue was derived[83]) caused great dissatisfaction. However, the opportunity had been given to the local colonists to frame their own constitution.[84] With this end in view discussions took place between 1851 and 1854 on the form which the new constitution would assume. Among the suggestions made were that in the new constitution a distinction should be made between bills of local concern and bills of Imperial concern and that the Governor should have no discretion to refuse assent to bills of the former class. Furthermore, it was urged that all revenue derived from the colony should be within the sole control of the New South Wales legislature. For this reason, it was proposed that the legislature itself should be completely responsible for the expenses of administration. Two Houses of Parliament were to be created; one a nominee house, the other elected by the inhabitants of the colony, and

[77] S. 14.
[78] S. 14.
[79] S. 18.
[80] S. 27. However, the local legislatures could not impose differential duties (s. 27) or duties on supplies imported for Her Majesty's forces or inconsistent with Imperial treaty obligations (s. 31).
[81] Which included the Northern Rivers District of New South Wales as well as Queensland.
[82] S. 34.
[83] It appeared that a major reason for the Imperial authorities retaining control over unalienated Crown lands was to assist the financing of migration to the colonies. See *New South Wales* v. *Commonwealth* (1976) 8 A.L.R. 1 at 13 (Barwick, C.J.).
[84] Subject to the requirement of reservation.

the voting qualifications were to be further liberalized.[85] At the end of 1853 a bill embodying these provisions was passed by the New South Wales Legislative Council and forwarded to England. Certain amendments were made by the Imperial Parliament including the omission of the clause which was intended to control the Governor in giving assent to bills. In its amended form it was passed as a schedule to "an Act to enable Her Majesty to assent to a Bill, as amended, of the Legislature of New South Wales, and to grant a Civil List to Her Majesty".[86] The ratification by the Imperial Parliament of the amended bill was necessary because the New South Wales legislature had in certain respects gone beyond its powers in drawing up the Constitution. Section 32 of the Australian Constitutions Act (No. 2) (the original enabling act) had merely given power to "establish instead of the legislative council, a council and a house of representatives, or other separate legislative houses, to consist respectively of such members, to be appointed or elected respectively by such persons and in such manner, as by such Act or Acts shall be determined, and to vest in such council and house of representatives or other separate legislative houses the powers and functions of the legislative council for which the same may be substituted". No power was given by this section to vest in the local legislature authority over Crown lands. Consequently a new enabling act had to be passed and to this new act the New South Wales Constitution Bill in its amended form was attached as a schedule. Subsequently it received the royal assent.[87]

The ultimate legal support for the New South Wales Constitution is therefore to be found in an Imperial enactment which, to distinguish it from the New South Wales Constitution Act which it sanctions, is referred to as the New South Wales Constitution *Statute*.[88] This statute empowered the Queen to assent to the reserved bill and repealed so much of the earlier constitutional legislation as was repugnant to the bill.[89] It vested in the New South Wales legislature control

---

[85] It was proposed that the Upper House should consist in the first instance of persons to be nominated by the Governor and on whom hereditary titles should be conferred. See Melbourne, *Early Constitutional Development in Australia*, p.401.
[86] 18 & 19 Vict., c.54. For a discussion of the events leading up to responsible government in New South Wales see C. H. Currey, "Responsible Government in New South Wales", 42 *Royal Australian Historical Society Journal* (1956), 97 *et seq*.; W. J. V. Windeyer, "Responsible Government", *ibid.* (1957), 257 *et seq*.
[87] On 16 July 1855. The old Legislative Council was dissolved in February 1856.
[88] It consists of nine sections as compared with the fifty-eight sections of the Constitution Act.
[89] Ss. 1, 2.

and administration of the Crown lands in the colony.[90] However, it continued the provision of the Australian Constitutions Acts of 1842 and 1850 which related to the giving and withholding of the royal assent.[91] By s. 4 of the Statute authority was given to the New South Wales legislature to alter or repeal any provisions of the reserved bill subject to any conditions imposed by the bill as to alteration (until such conditions had been repealed by the New South Wales legislature).[92] Section 7 of the Statute continued the provision of the Australian Constitutions Act (No. 2) empowering the Crown to separate and to erect into a new colony the northern part of New South Wales.

The New South Wales Constitution *Act* (which as we have pointed out was a schedule to this Imperial statute) substituted for the existing Legislative Council a bicameral legislature with power to make laws for the peace, welfare, and good government of the colony.[93] This legislature was to consist of a Legislative Council of not less than twenty-one members who were to be nominated by the Governor with the advice of the Executive Council (four-fifths of whom were not to hold any office of profit under the Crown except as military officers or retired military officers)[94] and a Legislative Assembly of fifty-four members elected according to a property or income qualification.[95] Provision was made for the legislature to alter electoral boundaries and the number of representatives in the Assembly with the proviso that passage of bills of this second class was subject to a requirement of a two-thirds majority of members of the Assembly.[96] Power was also given to the legislature to alter the provisions relating to the Legislative Council subject to a requirement of a two-thirds majority in both Houses, reservation for the royal assent and laying before the Imperial Parliament.[97] The duration of the Legislative Assembly was

---

[90] S. 3.
[91] By s. 36 of the Constitution Act bills altering the Constitution were to be passed with a two-thirds majority of both Houses and reserved for the royal assent.
[92] S. 1.
[93] S. 1.
[94] S. 2. The first members of the Council were to hold their seats for five years, but all future members were to hold their seats for life. See s. 33.
[95] S. 10. The main property qualifications which were set out in s. 11 were ownership of freehold of the value of £100 or occupancy of property which had an annual value of £10, or occupancy of a lodging or room at a price of £10 per annum. The income qualification was receipt of a salary of £100 per year. It must be pointed out that this property qualification was changed to one based on manhood suffrage soon after the advent of responsible government.
[96] S. 15.
[97] S. 36.

to be five years. Taxation and appropriation bills were to originate in the Assembly.[98]

Section 37 of the Act was a crucial section. It provided:

> The appointment to all public offices under the Governor hereafter to become vacant, or to be created, whether such offices be salaried or not, shall be vested in the Governor with the advice of the Executive Council with the exception of the appointment of officers liable to retire from office on political grounds which appointments shall be vested in the Governor alone....

The officers so liable to retire were the Attorney-General, the Solicitor-General, Colonial Secretary, Colonial Treasurer, and Auditor-General.[99] These officials (plus others not being more than five designated by the Governor) were exempted from the provision which disqualified persons holding any office of profit under the Crown from sitting in the Legislative Assembly.[100] The Act also made provision for the payment of pensions to the present incumbents of ministerial offices who were liable to retire on political grounds.[101] These provisions, read in conjunction with those provisions relating to the control of finance to be mentioned later, implicitly introduced the system of responsible government, viz. that when a change in the attitude of the legislature towards the Government occurred (as, for example, after an election) the members of the Government who did not have the confidence of the majority of members of the legislature were to resign and make way for ministers who did have this confidence. It was intended that this system should replace the existing system whereby the members of the executive held permanent posts by appointment of the Home Government, their salaries being guaranteed by Imperial legislation.[102]

In respect of particular legislative powers which were until 1855 denied to the New South Wales legislature the Act provided as follows. The legislature had the power of regulating the occupation of and sale of Crown lands.[103] It could impose customs duties on all goods except those introduced for consumption by the armed forces, but could not impose differential duties or duties which were opposed to Imperial

---

[98]S. 21.
[99]S. 51.
[100]S. 18.
[101]S. 51.
[102]For a discussion of the changeover to responsible government in New South Wales, see Melbourne, *Early Constitutional Development in Australia*, pp.427-32.
[103]S. 43.

treaty obligations.[104] A Consolidated Revenue Fund was established to comprise all revenue derived from the colony (including the casual revenues of the Crown) to be appropriated for the public service of the colony.[105] Provision was made for a Civil List for which certain sums were appropriated under three schedules: (1) salaries of the Governor, judiciary, and ministers; (2) pensions for the judiciary, ministers, and public servants; (3) public worship.[106] These sums were to be provided for out of the Consolidated Revenue Fund in return for the surrender by the Crown of all its revenues (territorial, casual, and otherwise) within the colony.[107] Although s. 54 provided that no bill should be passed appropriating money from the Consolidated Revenue Fund unless such bill "shall have first been recommended by a message of the Governor to the Legislative Assembly", it is clear that the adoption of the principle of responsible government implicit in the Constitution Act meant that the Governor would act according to the wishes of the legislature in this matter, i.e. he would act on the advice of ministers responsible to the legislature. Finally, by s. 58 the previous legislation applicable to the colony which was repugnant to the Act was repealed.[108]

At this stage we may summarize the development of the constitutional powers of the New South Wales Governors and legislatures from 1788 to 1855 when the colony acquired its first indigenous constitution. In the period between 1788 and 1823 New South Wales can best be described as a special type of Crown colony to which English law was applicable in a limited way in view of the penal nature of the settlement. Legislative (as well as executive) power was vested in the Governor as representative of the Crown (subject of course to the overriding supremacy of the Imperial legislature). While some writers have taken the view that the application of the civil law in the early years was unconstitutional because of lack of authorization in the Act of 1787, the better view is that the royal prerogative provided an adequate basis for the establishment of civil jurisdiction. In 1823 with the passing of the Act 4 Geo. IV, c.96, New South Wales became a colony

---

[104] Ss. 44, 45.
[105] S. 47.
[106] These sums were subject to modification by the local legislature subject only to the requirement of the reservation of bills which amended them.
[107] S. 50.
[108] At the same time by 18 & 19 Vict., c.56, the Imperial Legislature repealed the provisions of the Waste Lands Act which excluded the revenues of Crown land from local control.

in the real sense with a local legislature. However, the wide powers of enactment still vested in its Governor which might be exercised contrary to the wishes of the majority of the Council, including the sole right of initiating bills, showed that representative government was not contemplated at this time by the Home Government. However, a certain mitigation of these powers was effected in 1825 by the creation under the royal prerogative of an executive council to advise the Governor in the exercise of his powers. The passage of the Australian Courts Act in 1828 further limited the powers of the Governor in that he was deprived of the right to enact legislation contrary to the wishes of the majority of the Legislative Council. It also enlarged the size of the Council and so provided for the representation of a greater variety of views.

However, it was not until 1842 that provision was made for the establishment of representative government in New South Wales by the Australian Constitutions Act (No. 1). In that year the constitution of the colony underwent a radical reorganization with the creation of a legislature consisting of members of whom two-thirds were to be elected by inhabitants possessing certain property qualifications. The position of the Governor vis-a-vis the legislature was redefined: he was no longer a member of the legislature and so could not participate in its deliberations. He could not prevent the enactment of a bill except by the exercise of the prerogative right of withholding assent to a bill. However, the legislative powers of the Council were subject to certain restrictions in respect of the control of the local revenue, the revenue from Crown lands being entirely outside its jurisdiction.

The Australian Constitutions Act (No. 2) of 1850 gave to New South Wales and to the other Australian colonies (when they formed legislative councils similar to that of New South Wales, i.e. bodies consisting of elected and nominated members in the proportion of two to one) power to draw up their own constitution bills which were to be reserved for the royal assent. Pursuant to this enabling act the New South Wales Legislative Council passed a bill to establish a new constitution which was reserved for the royal assent. Certain amendments were made to it by the Imperial Government and in its modified form it was included as a schedule to an Imperial statute which authorized the Queen to assent to the bill in its amended form. This bill in its amended form became the New South Wales Constitution Act.

The New South Wales Constitution Statute (Imp.) of 1855 enlarged the legislative power of the colony by giving it power to control Crown lands, although it kept in force provisions of the Australian Constitutions Act relating to the reservation of certain types of bills. It empowered the New South Wales legislature to change its constitution if it desired (subject to fetters in the Constitution Act unless these were first repealed). The New South Wales Constitution Act established a bicameral legislature consisting of a nominated Council and an elected Assembly. This legislature was given power to make laws for the peace, welfare, and good government of the colony although there were certain limiting provisions. But the most important feature of the Act was that it ushered in the era of responsible government which was implicit in those provisions of the Act relating to the retirement of officers on political grounds. At this stage of its constitutional development New South Wales had a representative and responsible government. Its legislative powers were not however complete and it was subject of course to the overall supremacy of the Imperial Parliament.

CHAPTER TWO

The Other States

VICTORIA

SECTION 1 OF THE AUSTRALIAN CONSTITUTIONS ACT OF 1850 provided for the separation of the Port Phillip district from the territory of New South Wales. This separation was to take effect upon the issuing of writs for the election of members of the new legislature by the Governor and Legislative Council of New South Wales.[1] The Governor and Legislative Council of New South Wales were given the power to determine electoral boundaries within the new colony and the number of members of the legislature, subject to the proviso that the number of elected members to non-elected members was to be in the proportion of two to one.[2] On the issue of writs for the first election the colony of Victoria was to be established.[3] The electoral provisions as to qualifications of electors, etc., were to be the same as those in operation in New South Wales.[4] The Governor[5] and Legislative Council of Victoria were to have power to make laws for the peace, welfare, and good government of the colony subject to similar restrictions which were imposed on the New South Wales legislature, and had the same power to alter the constitution of the legislature and to substitute therefor a bicameral legislature.[6]

The Victorian Constitution Act was proclaimed and came into operation in January 1851, and the New South Wales legislature set to work to draw up an electoral system. The Act 14 Vict., No. 47 (N.S.W.) provided for a Legislative Council to consist of thirty members (twenty elected, ten nominated by the Governor). By 14 Vict., No. 44 (N.S.W.) the laws in force in New South Wales at the

---

[1] Under the 1842 Act the Port Phillip district elected six representatives to the New South Wales Legislative Council.
[2] S. 2.
[3] S. 5.
[4] S. 12.
[5] The Governor of Victoria, like the Governors of the other Australian colonies apart from New South Wales, was given the official title of Lieutenant-Governor, the Governor of New South Wales being titular head of the Australian colonies and holding the title of Governor-General. In actual fact, however, each representative of the Crown had ordinary gubernatorial powers within his area of jurisdiction.
[6] S. 14.

time of separation were to operate in Victoria. On 1 July 1851, the writs for the first election were issued and Victoria became a separate colony.[7] The new legislature set about its legislative programme and pursuant to the power conferred on it by the Australian Constitutions Act, passed a constitution bill which was reserved for the royal assent. The bill met with the same objections as had been directed against the New South Wales bill, viz. that in some respects it went beyond the power conferred by the enabling act.[8] The Home Government made a number of amendments to the bill which in its amended form was included in a schedule to an Imperial enactment which empowered Her Majesty "to assent to a Bill, as amended, of the Legislature of Victoria, to establish a Constitution in and for the Colony of Victoria".[9] As in the case of New South Wales, the ultimate authority of the Victorian Constitution is therefore to be found in an Imperial enactment. The Constitution Statute was similar to that relating to New South Wales and by s. 4 the Victorian legislature was empowered to alter the Constitution Act subject to conditions imposed as to alteration (unless these were previously repealed). The Victorian Constitution Act, however, departed in certain significant respects from the form of the New South Wales Act.

By s. 1 a Legislative Council and Assembly were substituted for the existing Council and power was given to the new body "to make laws in and for Victoria in all cases whatsoever".[10] Unlike the New South Wales Council the Victorian Council was to be an elected body. It was to consist of thirty members to be elected by inhabitants of the colony who possessed certain property or educational qualifications.[11] The Legislative Council could never be dissolved but members were to retire on a basis of rotation, five every second year, and their places

---

[7] For discussion of the first years of Victoria's existence as a separate colony, see E. Jenks, *The Government of Victoria* (London: Macmillan & Co., 1891), pp.150 *et seq.*; E. Sweetman, *Constitutional Development of Victoria* 1851-56 (Melbourne: Whitcombe & Tombs, 1921); J. Quick and R. R. Garran, *The Annotated Constitution of the Australian Commonwealth* (Sydney: Angus and Robertson, 1901), pp.51-58.
[8] For instance, in vesting in the local legislature control over Crown lands.
[9] 18 & 19 Vict., c.55.
[10] The phraseology "to make laws in and for Victoria in all cases whatsoever" does not seem to entail any significant legal difference as compared with the words used in the New South Wales Act where the power was "to make laws for the peace, welfare, and good government of New South Wales in all cases whatsoever". Implied in these grants of legislative power were restrictions based on the territorial scope of colonial statutes.
[11] Ss. 4, 5. The chief property qualifications were: ownership of a freehold of the value of £1,000, or of a five-year leasehold of a rent of £100. The educational qualifications were: graduate status, barrister or solicitor, medical practitioner, minister of religion, officer of Her Majesty's forces.

were to be filled in subsequent elections.[12] The Legislative Assembly was to consist of sixty members who also were to be elected by inhabitants possessing property qualifications less stringent than those required for the Council, and similar to those required for the electors of New South Wales.[13] The duration of the Assembly was to be five years.[14] All bills appropriating any part of the revenue or imposing any tax were to originate in the Assembly: such bills could be rejected but not altered by the Council.[15]

Restrictions on legislative power similar to those operating in New South Wales were imposed on the Victorian Parliament.[16] A Civil List was granted to the Crown (in schedules to the Act) in return for the surrender of Crown revenues which were transferred to the control of the legislature.[17] An interesting appropriation section to be found in the body of the Act itself was s. 53 which provided that £50,000 per year should be set aside for the advancement of the Christian religion in Victoria.[18] The Parliament was invested with power to alter the constitution of the Legislative Council or Assembly but it was provided that bills altering the constitution of the Council or Assembly or the Civil List schedules were not to become law unless the second and third readings had been passed by an absolute majority of the members of both the Council and Assembly and had been reserved for the royal assent.[19]

The doctrine of responsible government was recognized in three sections of the Act.[20] Appointments to public offices were vested in the Governor with the advice of the Executive Council, with the exception of appointments of officers liable to retire on political grounds which were vested in the Governor alone.[21] Provision was made for the payment of pensions to the present incumbents of offices who were liable to retire on these grounds.[22] On the other hand, the Victorian Act went beyond the New South Wales Act in expressly providing that a certain

---

[12]S. 3.
[13]Ss. 10, 12. Ownership of freehold estate of £50 or occupancy of a dwelling of the annual value of £10, or receipt of an annual salary of £100.
[14]S. 19.
[15]S. 56.
[16]I.e. as to customs legislation. Ss. 42, 43.
[17]Ss. 46, 47.
[18]Provision was made for the apportionment of this sum among all denominations.
[19]S. 60.
[20]Ss. 18, 37, 51.
[21]S. 37.
[22]S. 51.

number of responsible officers should be members of the legislature.[23] Section 18 provided that at least four of these officers should be members of the Council or Assembly.

Under the old system of government it was true that ministers were members of the legislature. But that did not *ipso facto* mean that they were responsible to the legislature. As has been pointed out earlier they held what in effect amounted to permanent appointments and were subject ultimately to the control of the Imperial Government (exercised through the Secretary of State for the Colonies and the Governor). They were appointed at the Governor's pleasure and could be dismissed by him, but such a dismissal would be subject to review by the Home authorities which could make an order of reinstatement.[24] Under the new system it was implied that the Governor would exercise his power of appointment and dismissal according to the wishes of the legislature, that ministerial positions were not permanent, and that an adverse vote on the part of the legislature against present ministers would lead to their release on political grounds. In the case of Victoria this understanding was strengthened by the formal requirement that at least four of these responsible ministers were to be members of the legislature.

Despite these provisions it must be pointed out that the operation of the doctrine of responsible government in the Australian colonies was based more on convention than on formal law. No obligation was imposed on the Governor to appoint the members of the ministry from the legislature but it was recognized that the administration of the affairs of the colony would very soon come to a halt if the ministry was elected in any other way.[25]

There is one further point to be considered at this stage. From what source did the Victorian (and New South Wales) Constitution derive its immediate force and validity? It seems that there are two alternatives: either from an enactment of the local legislature or from an enactment of the Imperial Legislature. The answer to the question it is submitted is to be found in the opinion of the law officers of Victoria (Mr. Stawell and Mr. Molesworth) laid before the Victorian Parliament in 1856: "We attribute its efficacy, not to the power of the Colonial but of the Imperial Legislature, and the assent given by Her

---

[23] The responsible officers listed were: the Colonial Secretary, the Attorney-General, the Colonial Treasurer, the Commissioner of Public Works, the Collector of Customs, the Surveyor-General, and the Solicitor-General.
[24] Jenks, *The Government of Victoria*, p.209.
[25] *Ibid.*, p.271.

Majesty in Council to the Bill as above amended."[26]

There is no doubt that had the Imperial Parliament introduced no amendments into the drafts of the bills as originally passed by New South Wales and Victoria there would have been no need for the sanction of Imperial legislation. However, this sanction was necessary as both bills had exceeded the powers conferred by the Australian Constitutions Act 1850, purporting, as they did, to repeal Imperial legislation. Any assent therefore given by Her Majesty to the bills in the form in which they were sent to England would have been null and void. There is also a second reason why the source of validity of the Victorian and New South Wales Constitutions must be sought in Imperial statutes. The Imperial Parliament made certain amendments to the draft constitution bills. The authority of the amendments and therefore of the bills as ultimlately assented to by the Queen is derived from this intervention on the part of the Imperial Parliament.[27] Consequently the immediate source of validity of the original Victorian and New South Wales Constitution Acts is to be found in Imperial statutes. As we shall see, the constitutions of the other Australian colonies came into existence in a different way.

SOUTH AUSTRALIA

Unlike the foundation of New South Wales, that of South Australia was the result of the endeavours of private citizens who were desirous that colonization would be the work of free immigrants and not of convicts.[28] As a consequence of the entreaties of a group called the South Australian Association which had been formed to develop the territory of South Australia, the Imperial Parliament in 1834 passed "an Act to empower his Majesty to erect South Australia into a British province or provinces, and to provide for the Colonization and Government thereof".[29] The constitutional significance of this Act lies in the fact that it did not establish a constitution but empowered the King in Council to take the necessary steps to establish a legislative body, the

[26] *Votes and Proceedings of the Victorian Legislative Council*, 1855-56, ii, p.783.
[27] On the other hand, Jenks considers that the failure of the Imperial Parliament itself to *enact* the terms of the amended draft meant that it did not take effect as an Imperial statute: *The Government of Victoria*, p.204.
[28] See B. T. Finnis, *Constitutional History of South Australia* 1836-57 (Adelaide: W. C. Rigby, 1886); E. Sweetman, *Australian Constitutional Development* (Melbourne: Macmillan & Co. and Melbourne University Press, 1925), pp.306 *et seq.*; G. D. Combe, *Responsible Government in South Australia* (Adelaide: Government Printer, 1957); Quick and Garran, *The Annotated Constitution of the Australian Commonwealth*, pp.62-67.
[29] 4 & 5 Will, IV, c.95.

enactments of which were to be subject to disallowance by the King in Council.

The Act empowered the King in Council to vest in one or more residents of the colony authority to make laws for the peace, order, and good government of the province.[30] Such laws were not to be contrary to any provision of the Act and were to be laid before the King in Council.[31] The remaining sections of the Act dealt with the organization of the land settlement programme. Authority was given to the King in Council to appoint three or more Commissioners to carry out this programme.[32] Provision was made for the erection by Order in Council of the province to an ordinary colony with its own constitution and legislature when the population numbered 50,000.[33] Pursuant to the Act, the province was founded in 1836 and a Governor, Commissioners, and other officials were appointed. Legislative power was vested in the Governor with the concurrence of the Chief Justice, the Colonial Secretary, and Attorney-General or two of them.[34]

In 1842 an Act of the Imperial Parliament was passed to provide for the "Better Government of South Australia".[35] This Act repealed the 1834 Act. Section 5 of the Act empowered the Queen in Council to constitute a legislative council to be composed of the Governor and seven other persons with authority to make laws for the peace, order, and good government of the colony. By s. 6 provision was made for the establishment by Her Majesty in the future of a bicameral legislature to consist of a General Assembly to be elected by the inhabitants and a Council of nominated members, or of a unicameral legislature to consist of elected and nominated members. Under s. 5 of the Act a Legislative Council was constituted consisting of the Governor, three official members, and four others to be nominated from the independent colonists. This of course meant that the Governor, by his casting vote, retained control over the legislative machinery of the colony. The Crown took no steps to implement s. 6.[36]

[30] Ss. 1, 2.
[31] S. 2.
[32] S. 3.
[33] S. 23.
[34] Quick and Garran, *The Annotated Constitution of the Australian Commonwealth*, p.63. Insofar as South Australia was founded in 1836, the reception of English law is to be dated from that year. See Acts Interpretation Act (S.A.) 1915, s. 48. However it has been argued that as the territory of South Australia was included within the colony of New South Wales, the reception of English law should be dated from 1828. See 23 *Australian Law Journal* (1949), 192.
[35] 5 & 6 Vict., c.61.
[36] The reason was that this provision was superseded by the Australian Constitutions Act of 1850.

When the Australian Constitutions Act of 1850 was enacted, the province of South Australia was included within its operation. The existing Council of South Australia was empowered to establish a Council consisting of not more than twenty-four members (a third of whom were to be nominated by the Crown, two-thirds elected by the inhabitants).[37] The various restrictions on legislative power applicable to New South Wales were extended to South Australia.[38] The new Legislative Council with which South Australia achieved representative government was constituted in July 1851.[39]

The Legislative Council of South Australia had power under s. 32 of the Australian Constitutions Act to alter its constitution and to substitute for the Council a bicameral legislature. Pursuant to this power the South Australian legislature passed a constitution bill providing for such a legislature. The bill also contained certain provisions vesting in the Privy Council jurisdiction to determine the validity of the exercise of the Governor's right of reserving bills and the monarch's right of disallowing bills. There was also a provision vesting powers over Crown lands in the legislature of the colony.[40] These provisions as we have seen went beyond the powers conferred by s. 32 which did not authorize legislation repealing Imperial legislation or restricting the royal prerogative. Consequently, when the bill reached England assent was not given to it and it was returned to the colony with information as to the fate that had befallen the New South Wales and Victorian bills. The Home Government had decided not to follow the precedent established in the cases of New South Wales and Victoria, namely, to amend the local enactments and to empower Her Majesty to assent to them in their amended form, but had transmitted the bill to South Australia for reconsideration.[41] In 1855 a new bill from which the objectionable provisions had been omitted was passed by the South Australian legislature and received the royal assent. This assent was given in 1856 and the Act was entitled The South Australian Constitution Act (No. 2, 1855-56).[42] The immediate source of validity therefore of the South Australian Constitution is to be found in an enactment of the local legislature.

[37] S. 7.
[38] Ss. 14, 31. These sections denied legislative power over Crown lands and certain types of customs duties.
[39] Quick and Garran, *The Annotated Constitution of the Australian Commonwealth*, p.64.
[40] See Sweetman, *Australian Constitutional Development*, pp.312-13.
[41] *Ibid.*, pp.315-16.
[42] *Ibid.*, p.318. It was not until 1857, however, the the term of the old Legislative Council expired and elections were held under the new Act.

This Act established a Legislative Council and House of Assembly as component parts of the legislature in which were reposed the powers of the existing Legislative Council.[43] The new Legislative Council was to consist of eighteen members elected by inhabitants having property qualifications. Members were to retire on a basis of rotation, six every four years.[44] The House of Assembly, the duration of which was to be three years, was to be elected by adult male suffrage.[45] All money bills were to originate in the House of Assembly.[46] An interesting section of the South Australian Constitution Act was s. 28 which allowed the Governor to transmit a message to the Council or Assembly suggesting any amendment to a bill presented to him for the royal assent and required the Houses to take such a message into consideration in accordance with Standing Orders.

The South Australian Parliament was given full power to repeal or alter any provision of the Constitution Act subject to the proviso that any bill effecting an alteration in the constitution of the Legislative Council or House of Assembly was to be passed at the second and third sittings by an absolute majority of the members of both Houses and to be reserved for the royal assent.[47]

The doctrine of responsible government was recognized in the requirement that five principal ministers of the Crown[48] could not continue in office if they did not hold a seat in Parliament within three months of the first general election.[49] The appointment of these officers was vested in the Governor alone.[50] Compensation was to be paid to the present incumbents of ministerial posts who were liable to loss of office "by reason of their inability to become ministers of parliament or to command the support of a majority of members".[51] The doctrine of responsible government was therefore written into the South Australian Constitution to a much greater extent than in the New South Wales and Victorian Constitutions.

---

[43] S. 1.
[44] Ss. 5, 6, 8. The property qualifications were: ownership of a freehold of the value of £50, or a leasehold of an annual value of £20, or occupancy of a dwellinghouse of an annual value of £25.
[45] Ss. 3, 16.
[46] S. 1.
[47] S. 34.
[48] The Chief Secretary, Attorney-General, Treasurer, Commissioner of Crown Lands, Commissioner of Public Works.
[49] S. 32.
[50] S. 29.

TASMANIA

The constitutional history of Van Diemen's Land[52] was associated with that of New South Wales for a considerable period of time. From 1803, when it was settled, to 1823, it was within the legislative jurisdiction of the Governor of New South Wales and from 1823 to 1825 within the jurisdiction of the Governor and Legislative Council of New South Wales.[53] Some doubts had been expressed about the validity of the exercise of criminal jurisdiction within the territory as the Act of 1787 had merely empowered the King to establish a criminal judicature in New South Wales and "the islands adjacent". Be that as it may the affairs of the colony continued to be administered from Sydney,[54] and it is therefore clear that Van Diemen's Land was considered to be an adjacent island. The Act of 1823 by s. 44 gave the Crown power by Order in Council to separate Van Diemen's Land from New South Wales and to establish in the new colony a legislative and administrative structure similar to that of New South Wales. In 1825 this separation occurred with the formation of Legislative and Executive councils on the New South Wales pattern.[55] The Act of 1828 was also extended to Van Diemen's Land so that from 1828 onwards the colony had a constitution similar to that of New South Wales.[56] The 1842 Act which conferred representative government on New South Wales was not extended to the island colony. The reason given was the continuance of transportation to the colony.[57] However, the Australian Constitutions Act of 1850 empowered the existing Council to establish a new Council to consist of twenty-four persons of whom one-third were to be nominated by the Crown and two-thirds elected by the inhabitants, and this new body was given power to alter the constitution and to substitute for itself a bicameral legislature.[58] Pursuant to these enabling provisions the new Council in 1854 enacted a constitution bill which was transmitted to England for the royal assent. The bill, which had not, as in the case of the other colonies, ex-

---

[51]S. 39.
[52]Quick and Garran, *The Annotated Constitution of the Australian Commonwealth,* pp.58-62. It was not until 1853 that the name of the colony was changed to Tasmania.
[53]Sweetman, *Australian Constitutional Development,* pp.320-21.
[54]Under the local supervision of a Lieutenant-Governor.
[55]Quick and Garran, *The Annotated Constitution of the Australian Commonwealth,* p. 59.
[56]Sweetman, *Australian Constitutional Development,* pp.321-22.
[57]*Ibid.,* p.322. See also W. A. Townsley, *The Struggle for Self-Government in Tasmania* 1842-1856 (Hobart: Government Printer, 1951).
[58]S. 7.

ceeded the powers conferred by the 1850 Act, received the royal assent.[59] Its immediate validity therefore rests on local enactment.

The Tasmanian Constitution Act established a Legislative Council and a House of Assembly. The Legislative Council was to consist of fifteen members who were to retire on a basis of rotation, five every three years.[60] They were to be elected by inhabitants possessing property or educational qualifications.[61] The House of Assembly, the duration of which was to be five years,[62] was to be elected by inhabitants possessing property or educational qualifications.[63] It was to consist of thirty members.[64] Bills for appropriating revenue or for imposing any tax were to originate in the Assembly.[65] Responsible government was implicit in the Constitution Act in the reference to the liability of the present incumbents of ministerial positions to retirement or dismissal on political grounds,[66] and provision was made for the payment of compensation in the event of this happening.[67]

One feature of the Tasmanian Constitution Act which distinguishes it from the other acts is that it is incomplete. There are no provisions in the Act which empower the legislature to make laws for the peace, welfare, and good government of the colony or enable it to change its constitution. The Act must therefore be read in conjunction with those provisions of the Australian Constitutions Act (No. 2) which conferred law-making power, including the power of constitutional alteration.[68]

QUEENSLAND

In s. 51 of the Australian Constitutions Act of 1842, power was given to the Queen to erect into a separate colony territory in New South Wales lying northward of the twenty-sixth degree of south latitude. The size of this territory was increased by the Australian

[59] 18 Vict., No. 17. Sweetman, *Australian Constitutional Development*, p.328.
[60] Ss. 6, 9.
[61] S. 6. Qualifications: ownership of freehold of annual value of £50, graduate status, barrister or solicitor, medical practitioner, minister of religion, officer of Her Majesty's forces.
[62] S. 16.
[63] Ownership of a freehold estate of £100, or occupancy of a dwelling of an annual value of £10, or receipt of salary of £100, or possession of the educational qualifications as for the Legislative Council.
[64] S. 15.
[65] S. 33.
[66] S. 32.
[67] S. 32.
[68] Quick and Garran, *The Annotated Constitution of the Australian Commonwealth*, p.61. The sections in question are ss. 14 and 32.

Constitutions Act of 1850 which set the dividing line at the thirtieth degree of south latitude. Separation might be effected on the petition of the inhabitant householders of the area above this latitude.[69] This power was continued by the New South Wales Constitution Statute which empowered the Queen to separate the territory referred to and to make provision by Order in Council for the government of the colony which was to resemble the government and legislature established in New South Wales at this time.[70] The inhabitants of the northern part of New South Wales—the Moreton Bay district—had for some years been electing representatives to the New South Wales legislature.[71] In 1856 the representatives so elected numbered nine. Several petitions for separation were presented and in 1859 letters patent were issued erecting the territory into a colony under the name of Queensland, the southern boundary being a line commencing on the eastern coastline at latitude 28° 8'.[72] At the same time an Order in Council was made providing for the constitution of the new colony.[73]

The Order in Council, the authority of which was derived from s. 7 of the New South Wales Constitution Statute, was broadly similar to the New South Wales Constitution. It made provision for a Legislative Council and Assembly and power was given to the Queen with the advice of the legislature to make laws for the peace, welfare, and good government of the colony.[74] The Governor of New South Wales was authorized to take the initial steps in the formation of the Council and Assembly.[75] The Council was to consist of members summoned by the Governor, four-fifths of whom were to hold no office of profit under the Crown.[76] Those members first summoned were to hold their seats for five years; all future members were to have a life tenure.[77] The Legislative Assembly, the duration of which was to be five years,[78]

[69] S. 34.
[70] S. 7.
[71] Sweetman, *Australian Constitutional Development*, pp.331 *et seq.*
[72] By letters patent of 1872 and 1878 and the Queensland Coast Islands Act of 1879 provision was made for the annexation of islands in the Torres Strait to Queensland. See R. D. Lumb, *The Maritime Boundaries of Queensland and New South Wales*, University of Queensland Faculty of Law Paper, Vol. I, No. 4, 1964. On the validity of the letters patent see *R. v. Gomez* (1880) 5 Q.S.C.R. 189. *Cantley v. State of Queensland* (1973) 47 A.L.J.R. 538.
[73] "Order in Council empowering the Governor of Queensland to make laws, and to provide for the Administration of Justice in the said colony." *Queensland Government Gazette*, I, 1859-60, 7.
[74] S. 2.
[75] Ss. 3, 5.
[76] S. 3.
[77] S. 4.
[78] S. 7.

was to be elected in accordance with the qualifications pertaining to the election of members of the New South Wales Assembly which were prescribed by the New South Wales Constitution Act in its original form (until these qualifications were amended by the Queensland Legislature).[79] The limitations on the legislative power of the other colonies were extended to Queensland[80] but, as in their case, the Queensland legislature was to have the control of Crown lands.[81] The financial provisions of the New South Wales Act were also extended to Queensland.[82] The Queensland legislature was also given power to alter any provision of the Order in Council apart from those provisions of the earlier acts embodied in the Order requiring the reservation of bills of a certain nature for the royal assent. Any bill altering the constitution of the Council in such a way as to make it an elective body was to be laid before the Imperial Parliament for thirty days and reserved for the royal assent.[83]

Although New South Wales had introduced manhood suffrage in substitution for the property qualifications for its Legislative Assembly before 1859, the qualifications for the Queensland Legislative Assembly were drawn up on a property basis and because of doubts that had arisen as to the validity of this provision relating to electoral qualifications—the qualifications of members of the two legislatures not being similar—the Imperial Parliament passed an Act (24 & 25 Vict., c.44) validating those clauses of the Order in Council which made provision for the application to Queensland of the qualifications of electors under New South Wales law as they existed in 1856 and not in 1859.

In 1867 the Queensland Parliament, pursuant to the power conferred upon it by the Order in Council, passed "an Act to Consolidate the Laws relating to the Constitution of the Colony of Queensland.".[84] This Act re-enacted the applicable sections of the New South Wales Constitution Act and the Order in Council and incorporated Queensland constitutional legislation passed between 1860 and 1867.[85]

---

[79] S. 8.
[80] Ss. 18, 19 (with respect to customs duties).
[81] S. 17, referring to the repeal of the Waste Lands Act.
[82] S. 21.
[83] S. 22.
[84] 31 Vict., No. 38.
[85] I.e. Queensland legislation relation to the Council and Assembly which had been formed in the first place as we have seen by the Governor of New South Wales according to the terms of the Order in Council.

WESTERN AUSTRALIA

Western Australia had its constitutional origin in an Imperial Act of 1829—"An Act to provide until the 31st December, 1834, for the government of Her Majesty's settlement of Western Australia on the western coast of New Holland."[86] This Act empowered the Crown to authorize any three or more persons to make laws for the colony.[87] Such laws, which were first to be proposed by the Governor of the colony, were to be laid before both Houses of the Imperial Parliament and were subject to disallowance.[88] In 1830 an Order in Council was made which set up a Legislative Council consisting of the Governor (Stirling) and four official nominees. Under the Order in Council legislation could only be proposed by the Governor. This Order in Council was dispatched to Western Australia in 1831 together with a Commission appointing Stirling as Governor[89] and Instructions to the Governor. These Instructions established an Executive Council (consisting of the same nominess as were to sit in the Legislative Council). However it was not until 1832 that appointments were made to both bodies. At a later date four unofficial members were added to the Legislative Council.[90]

Although the constitutional provisions of the 1829 Act were meant to be temporary, Western Australia did not reap the benefits conferred on the other colonies until a late stage in its development. The Australian Constitutions Act of 1850 by s. 9 provided that, upon the petition of not less than one-third of the householders of the colony, a Legislative Council (to consist of members of whom two-thirds would be elected) might be established by the existing Council. The other provisions of the 1850 Act were to be applicable to the new Council when established. In 1865 a householders' petition was presented to the legislature requesting a Council as contemplated by s. 9, but it was rejected. However, the existing Council agreed to the addition of further non-official members to their body and the Governor agreed to nominate to the Council six members who were elected by the popula-

---

[86] 10 Geo. IV, c.22. For circumstances surrounding the foundation of the colony, see J. Battye, *Western Australia* (Oxford: Clarendon Press, 1924), pp.74 *et seq.*; Quick and Garran, *The Annotated Constitution of the Australian Commonwealth*, pp.67-71.

[87] Sweetman, *Australian Constitutional Development*, p.337.

[88] *Ibid.*, p.338.

[89] Previous to this Stirling had carried out his duties under Instructions issued in 1828.

[90] Sweetman, *Australian Constitutional Development*, p.339.

tion on an adult male suffrage basis.[91] Between 1868 and 1870 the
Council consisted of an equal number of official and non-official
members.[92] With the cessation of transportation to the colony in 1869,
attempts were made to secure representative government and a further
petition was presented. At last the Western Australian Legislative
Council decided to implement the provisions of s. 9 of the Australian
Constitutions Act (No. 2) and enacted a bill to provide for a Council
to consist of eighteen members, six of whom were to be appointed by
the Crown and the remainder elected by the inhabitants.[93] But twenty
more years were to elapse before the advent of a bicameral legislature
and responsible government. In 1889 the Western Australian Parliament, pursuant to power conferred upon it by s. 32 of the Australian
Constitutions Act of 1850, passed a constitution bill which was
reserved for the royal assent. Since the bill exceeded the powers conferred by s. 32[94] it was necessary for it to be ratified by the Imperial
Parliament, and in 1890 the Imperial Parliament passed an Act to
enable the Queen to assent to a bill for the conferring of a Constitution
on Western Australia.[95] The reserved bill was included in a schedule to
this statute. The statute repealed earlier Imperial legislation inconsistent with the provisions of the bill but retained those provisions which
related to the reservation of bills for the royal assent.[96] It vested control of Crown lands in the legislature of the colony[97] and empowered it
to alter any provisions of the reserved bill.[98]

The Western Australian Constitution Act[99] established a bicameral
legislature with power to make laws for the peace, order, and good
government of the colony. The Legislative Council was to consist of
fifteen members nominated by the Governor[100] who had a tenure subject to the following conditions. On the expiration of six years, or when

---

[91] Battye, *Western Australia*, p.277.
[92] *Ibid.*, p.278.
[93] "An Ordinance to provide for the establishment of a Legislative Council, the division of the colony into electoral districts, and the election of members to serve in such
Council." No. 13 of 1870.
[94] S. 3 of the bill purported to vest control of Crown lands southward of a certain
latitude in the Western Australian legislature. The Waste Lands Repeal Act of 1855
had not been extended to Western Australia.
[95] 53 & 54 Vict. (Imp.), c.26.
[96] S. 2.
[97] S. 3.
[98] S. 5. Section 6 of the Act empowered the Queen by Order in Council to divide the
colony by separation of the northern part thereof. This section became inoperative on
the enactment of the Commonwealth Constitution Act.
[99] The reserved bill.
[100] S. 6.

the population should have reached 60,000 (whichever should first happen), the Council was to become an elective body the members of which were to be elected by inhabitants having property qualifications.[101] The Legislative Assembly, which was to have a duration of four years,[102] was to consist of thirty members elected by inhabitants possessing property qualifications.[103] Certain restrictions were imposed on the powers of the legislature.[104] The legislature was given power to appropriate funds from the Consolidated Revenue subject, *inter alia*, to the charges imposed by the provisions of the Civil List.[105] It could alter any section of the Act, including the provisions of the Civil List, subject to the provisos that alterations to the constitution of the Council or Assembly should be effected by an absolute majority of members of both Houses and that bills affecting the charges on Consolidated Revenue should be reserved.[106] The doctrine of responsible government was implicitly recognized in the sections which vested appointment of officers liable to retire on political grounds in the Governor and made provision for the payment of compensation to present incumbents so liable to retire.[107] An important section in the Act was s. 70 under which the right of the aboriginal race to a share in the appropriations from the Consolidated Revenue Fund was recognized.[108]

In 1893, the population of Western Australia having reached 60,000 an act was passed abolishing the nominee Council and substituting for it an elective Council to consist of twenty-one members, seven of whom were to retire every two years, elected by inhabitants possessing a property qualification.[109] At the same time the constitu-

---

[101] S. 42. Qualifications of electors: ownership of freehold estate of the value of £200, or a leasehold estate of an annual value of £30, or occupancy of a dwelling-house of an annual value of £30.

[102] S. 14.

[103] Ss. 11, 39. Electoral qualifications: ownership of a freehold estate of £100, or a leasehold estate of an annual value of £10, or occupancy of a dwelling-house or rooms of annual value of £10.

[104] Customs duties were not to be differential or imposed on goods imported for Her Majesty's forces or to be inconsistent with Imperial treaty obligations. Ss. 59, 60.

[105] Ss. 64, 69. See also s. 70.

[106] S. 73.

[107] Ss. 74, 71.

[108] For the subsequent history of amendments to this section see Act No. 14 of 1905, s. 65.

[109] The Constitution Amendment Act 57 Vict., No. 14, ss. 4, 8, 12. Qualifications: ownership of a freehold estate of £100, or a leasehold estate of at least 18 months' duration of an annual value of £25, or occupancy of a dwelling house of an annual value of £25, or registration on the electoral lists of municipalities in respect of property rated at £25.

tion of the Assembly was changed-it was to consist of thirty-three members to be elected by inhabitants with less stringent property qualifications.[110] Finally, in 1899, the Western Australian Parliament passed a Constitution Act to amend and consolidate the previous enactments.[111] This Act introduced a number of changes in the Constitution of the colony.[112] As it stood, however, prior to its consolidation, the Western Australian Constitution derived its immediate force from an Imperial enactment. It had in this respect therefore a closer affinity with the Constitutions of Victoria, New South Wales, and Queensland than with those of South Australia and Tasmania.

SUMMARY

In conclusion we may summarize the characteristic features of the Constitution Acts of the Australian colonies in their original form. The Australian Constitutions Act of 1850 may be regarded as the initial charter of self-government for the colonies. Section 32 of that Act empowered all those colonies which possessed a Legislative Council, a majority of the members of which were elected by the inhabitants, to establish bicameral legislatures. At that time only New South Wales fulfilled this condition. The Act, however, as we have seen, made provision for the separation of Victoria from New South Wales and for the establishment of a Legislative Council similar in structure to that of New South Wales. It also empowered the Legislative Councils of South Australia and Tasmania—which were not representative bodies—to create Councils of a representative nature. In 1851 South Australia and Tasmania brought into existence Councils of the nature specified (two-thirds of the members were to be elected, and one-third nominated) and therefore from that time could exercise the power conferred by s. 32 to establish bicameral legislatures. Queensland of course, which did not fall within these provisions, was separated from New South Wales in 1859 by an Order in Council which made provision for a bicameral legislature. It was not until 1870 that Western Australia fulfilled the conditions of the Australian Constitutions Act

---

[110]Ss. 15, 21. Qualifications: ownership of a freehold of £50, or a leasehold of an annual value of £10, or occupancy of a dwelling-house of an annual value of £10, or registration on the electoral lists of municipalities in respect of property.
[111]Western Australian Constitution Acts Amendment Act, No. 19, of 1899.
[112]It increased the number of Legislative Councillors to thirty and reduced the property qualifications of electors. The size of the Legislative Assembly was increased to fifty and its duration shortened to three years. Provision was made for the appointment of six principal executive officers of government who were liable to retire on political grounds.

for acquiring a representative Legislative Council and twenty more years were to elapse before steps were taken to establish a bicameral legislature and responsible government under the enabling provision of the 1850 Act.

The various legislatures set to work to draw up constitutions pursuant to the power conferred by s. 32. In the case of three colonies—New South Wales, Victoria, and later Western Australia—the existing legislatures went beyond the power conferred by this section and vested in the new legislative bodies powers which were not authorized by that section. Some of the provisions of the reserved constitution bills which erred in this way were rejected by the Imperial Parliament (those purporting to restrict the Governor in the exercise of his discretion to assent to bills) while others were accepted (those vesting in the local legislatures control over Crown lands). It was therefore necessary for the Imperial Parliament to enact fresh legislation to validate the entire bills. In the case of South Australia and Tasmania the offending provisions were not included in their bills in their final form and the Imperial Parliament had by separate enactment vested in the new Australian legislatures control over Crown lands. It was not necessary therefore for those bills to be ratified by the Imperial Parliament. The Constitution of Queensland in its original form had a complete Imperial origin—the Order in Council of 1859.

The electoral structure of the Houses of the new legislatures differed in certain important respects. Qualifications of electors for the New South Wales, Victorian, Tasmanian, Queensland, and Western Australian Assemblies were based originally on ownership or occupation of property, while adult male suffrage was applicable to the South Australian Assembly. The duration of these Assemblies varied from three to five years. The Legislative Councils of New South Wales, Queensland, and Western Australia in their original form consisted of members appointed by the Crown; those of Victoria, South Australia, and Tasmania of members elected by inhabitants possessing property or educational qualifications.

The doctrine of responsible government was implicit in all the constitutions in those sections providing for the retirement of officers of government on political grounds and in the provisions giving the legislatures control over expenditure. In the case of two of the colonies—Victoria and South Australia—the doctrine was more adequately expressed in the requirement that certain ministers should hold seats in Parliament.

All the Constitution Acts (except that of Tasmania) vested in the new legislatures general legislative power as well as the specific power to amend their consitutions.[113] In some cases, however, bills affecting the constitution of the legislature were subject to the requirement that they be passed with certain majorities: all such bills were to be reserved by the Governor for the royal assent. Certain restrictions on substantive law-making power were also imposed: the legislatures could not impose certain types of customs duties. Besides constitution bills, certain other classes of bills were to be reserved for the royal assent.[114] Quite apart from these specific provisions the Imperial Parliament retained ultimate sovereignty over the Australian colonies with the consequence that Imperial legislation of paramount force (i.e. legislation applying to the colonies expressly or by necessary implication) prevailed over inconsistent local legislation.[115] The local legislatures also were subject to the limitation implied in the grant of legislative power by the Imperial Parliament that this power could not be exercised in such a way as to have an extraterritorial effect.[116]

A NOTE ON BOUNDARIES

The boundaries of New South Wales as designated in the Commission to Governor Phillip extended from Cape York to the southern coast of Tasmania and embraced all the country inland to the west as far as the 135th degree of east longitude and included the adjacent islands in the Pacific Ocean.[117] The western boundary was extended to the 129th meridian in 1825. In that year also Tasmania was separated from New South Wales and all islands south of Wilson's Promontory, as well as Macquarie Island, were included in the boundaries of the new colony. The boundaries of Western Australia, which was founded in 1829, extended from the western coastline to the 129th degree of longitude and included the adjacent islands in the Indian and Southern

[113] The source of Tasmanian general legislative power and specific power of constitutional alteration is to be found in ss. 14 and 32 of the Australian Constitutions Act of 1850. The South Australian Constitution Act, s. 5, conferred on the new council in South Australia the powers possessed by the old council under s. 14 of the Australian Constitutions Act.
[114] As required by the Australian Constitutions Acts of 1842 and 1850.
[115] See A. B. Keith, *Responsible Government in the Dominions* (2nd ed.; Oxford: Clarendon Press, 1928), I, 339-49.
[116] *Ibid.*, pp.321-38.
[117] For a discussion of the boundaries of the Australian colonies see F.W.S. Cumbrae-Stewart, *Australian Boundaries* (Brisbane: University of Queensland, 1934), republished in 5 *University of Queensland Law Journal* (1965). See also *New South Wales* v. *Commonwealth* (1976) 8 A.L.R.1 at 82-84 (Mason, J.), 99-103 (Jacobs, J.).

Oceans. The letters patent of 1836 which established the Province of South Australia defined the boundaries of that colony as including the territory bounded on the north by the 26th degree of south latitude, on the south by the Indian Ocean, on the west by the 132nd degree of longitude, and on the east by the 141st degree of longitude, together with adjacent islands. In 1851 with the separation of Victoria from New South Wales the boundary line between the two colonies was declared to be a line drawn from Cape Howe to the nearest source of the River Murray and by the course of that river to the eastern boundary of South Australia. It was further provided in the New South Wales Constitution Act of 1855 that the whole watercourse of the Murray was deemed to be within the territory of New South Wales. Finally, on the separation of Queensland from New South Wales in 1859, the land boundary between those colonies was defined as a line commencing about *28* degrees south latitude on the eastern coastline and following certain natural geographical features to the 29th parallel of south latitude and then in a straight line to the 141st meridian of the east longitude (the boundary of South Australia), together with adjacent islands in the Pacific.

The boundaries as thus defined had given rise to an anomalous position whereby a strip of territory of New South Wales was left between the boundaries of Western Australia and South Australia. The position was remedied by the Australian Colonies Act of 1861[118] and letters patent issued under that Act. In the first place, the territory of New South Wales which lay south of the 26th degree of south latitude between the eastern boundary of Western Australia and the western boundary of South Australia was detached from New South Wales and annexed to South Australia. Secondly, the area of New South Wales lying between the 141st and 138th meridians of east longitude was attached to Queensland, together with adjacent islands in the Gulf of Carpentaria. Thirdly, the remaining part of New South Wales lying north of the 26th degree of south latitude (between 129 degrees and 138 degrees of east longitude) was annexed to South Australia. This area was known as the Northern Territory and became a Commonwealth territory in 1911.

The maritime boundaries of Queensland were also left in an uncertain state after 1859 and it appeared that islands lying outside the three mile limit in the Pacific Ocean still remained with New South Wales.

[118] 24 & 25 Vict., c.44.

Letters patent of 1872 authorized the annexation to Queensland of islands within sixty miles of the coastline and further letters patent of 1878, which were followed by the Queensland Coast Islands Act of 1879, annexed to Queensland all islands lying within the Barrier Reef and in Torres Strait.[119] Islands lying outside the Barrier Reef have been constituted a federal territory under the Coral Seas Islands Act.[120]

---

[119] See Lumb, *The Maritime Boundaries of Queensland of New South Wales.* On the validity of the letters patent see *R.* v. *Gomez* (1880) 5 Q.S.C.R. 189. *Cantley* v. *State of Queensland* (1973) 47 A.L.J.R. 538.
[120] No. 58, of 1969.

PART II

The Present Structure of the Constitutions of the Australian States

PART II

The Present Structure of the Classification of the
Australian States

Introductory Note

THE NEW SOUTH WALES CONSTITUTION is embodied in the New South Wales Constitution Act of 1902 (No. 32) as amended, which repealed the 1855 Act. In 1975 the Victorian Parliament passed a Constitution Act to re-enact with additions and amendments the provisions of the earlier legislation (the Constitution Act of 1855 and the Constitution Act Amendment Act of 1958 (No. 6224)). The Act will be referred to as the Victorian Constitution Act, 1975. In Tasmania the original Constitution Act was repealed in 1934 and the Constitution is now set out in the Constitution Act (No. 94, 1934) as amended, while in South Australia also the original Constitution Act has been repealed and the Constitution is now embodied in the Constitution Act (No. 2151, 1934) as amended. In Queensland the Constitution Act of 1867 as amended is still in force. In Western Australia the Constitution Act of 1890 and the Constitution Acts Amendment Act of 1899, both as amended, remain in force. It can be seen therefore that today the Constitution Acts of New South Wales, Victoria, South Australia, and Queensland derive their immediate validity from local enactment; while the Constitution of Western Australia rests partially on an Imperial enactment. The Tasmanian Constitution, which is incomplete and must be read in conjunction with the law-making power conferred by the Australian Constitutions Act of 1850, is also partially based on Imperial enactment.

CHAPTER THREE

The Legislature

Legislative power in the Australian States is formally vested in a Legislature or Parliament which consists of the Queen (in Tasmania and South Australia, the Governor) and, with the exception of Queensland where the Upper House has been abolished, two Houses.[1] The Lower House is known as the Legislative Assembly in New South Wales, Queensland, Victoria and Western Australia and as the House of Assembly in South Australia and Tasmania. The Upper House is known in all States as the Legislative Council. In Queensland legislative power is vested in the Queen and the Legislative Assembly. In each State the Governor exercises the royal prerogative of assenting to bills passed by the Parliament although he must reserve bills of a certain nature for the royal assent.[2]

As we have seen, the system introduced by the Constitution Acts of the eighteen-fifties was, in the case of the majority of the colonial Lower Houses, one based on election by inhabitants having property qualifications, while the members of the Upper Houses were either nominated or elected by inhabitants having educational or higher property qualifications.[3] Over the years the property franchise for the Lower Houses has been abolished and one of adult suffrage has taken its place (subject of course to residential and citizenship qualifications being fulfilled). The nominated Upper House of Western Australia was converted into an elective body a few years after the grant of self-government to that colony,[4] while the nominated Upper House of New South Wales became an elective body in 1933.[5] The Upper House of Queensland was abolished in 1922.[6] The requirement in South Australia that members of the Upper House be at least thirty years of age was abolished in 1973 with the reduction of the voting and membership age to eighteen years of age.[7]

---

[1] C.A. (N.S.W.), s. 3 (C.A.—Constitution Act). C.A. (Vic.), s. 1. CA. (S.A.), s. 4. C.A. (Tas), s. 10. CA. (W.A.), s. 2. CA. (Qld.), s. 2.
[2] See pp.71-72.
[3] See p.41.
[4] 57 Vict., No. 14.
[5] Act No. 2, 1933.
[6] Constitution Amendment Act 12 Geo. V., No. 32.
[7] C.A. s.12 (as amended by Act No. 52 of 1973, s.6).

The minimum voting and membership age in the other States has also been reduced from twenty-one to eighteen years of age.

THE LOWER HOUSE

The structure is as follows. In New South Wales the Legislative Assembly consists of ninety-nine members who are elected by adult suffrage. Its duration is three years.[8] In Victoria the Assembly consists of eighty-one members elected by adult suffrage. Its duration is also three years.[9] South Australia has a House of Assembly which consists of forty-seven members elected by adult suffrage.[10] The duration of the Assembly is three years.[11]

Tasmania has a House of Assembly of thirty-five members (with five electoral districts returning seven members each under a system of proportional representation) elected by adult suffrage.[12] The duration of the Assembly is four years.[13] An interesting experiment was attempted in Tasmania to resolve deadlocks in the Assembly which until 1958 consisted of thirty members. It was to be found in s. 24A of the Constitution Act (repealed in 1958).[14] This section was inserted in the Constitution Act in 1953 and provided for the appointment of an additional member to the Assembly in the event of an equal number of members being elected who represented two opposing political parties (that is to say, fifteen members of one party and fifteen members of the other). In such a case the unsuccessful candidate belonging to the political party which had obtained the greatest number of votes in any of the divisions, i.e. more votes than any other defeated candidate, was to be declared elected to the Assembly. This would give the party that had obtained the greatest number of votes a majority of one. When this procedure proved unsatisfactory, an amendment was made in

[8]C.A., s. 24. Parliamentary Electorates and Elections Act (1912) as amended by Act No. 44 of 1973. In the case of New South Wales and the other States, the duration of the Assembly is subject to the possibility of prior dissolution.
[9]C.A., ss. 34, 35, 38. Electoral Provinces and Districts Act No. 8628 of 1974, s. 18 (2).
[10]C.A., ss. 27, 33. The C.A. Amendment Act No. 122 of 1975, s. 7, lays down rules relating to electoral redistributions and the division of the State into electoral districts including provision for the determination of a quota of electors with a permissible tolerance of ten percent. These rules are entrenched by the requirement that they shall not amended except by a Bill which has been submitted for approval at a referendum of electors for the House of Assembly.
[11]C.A., ss. 28.
[12]C.A., s. 22 (amended by s. 2 of Act No. 91 of 1958); s. 29.
[13]The term is to apply from the next House of Assembly election: C.A. s. 23 (as amended Act No. 79 of 1972).
[14]Inserted by Act No. 89 of 1953, s. 3.

1954 and an entirely different procedure was substituted for resolving Assembly deadlocks occurring when an equal number of members representing two opposing political parties was returned.[15] According to this procedure, the minority party (i.e. the party which had secured the smaller number of total votes) was given the right to elect a Speaker. If it did not avail itself of this right, the majority party was entitled to elect a Speaker from the ranks of the majority party and to have the Speaker so elected replaced by a member of its party. Here again the intention was to give the party obtaining the greatest number of votes in an election a majority of members in the event of a deadlock of the nature specified occurring. This provision was repealed in 1958 when the number of members of the Assembly was increased to an uneven number—thirty-five.[16]

The Queensland Legislative Assembly consists of eighty-two members elected by adult suffrage. The duration of the Assembly is three years.[17] In Western Australia, the Assembly consists of fifty-one members (increased to fifty-five members at the election next after December 1976)[18] elected by adult suffrage. Its duration is three years.[19]

THE UPPER HOUSE

The Legislative Council in all the States, subject to deadlock provisions, cannot be dissolved.[20] The method of electing members varies from State to State. In New South Wales the Legislative Council, which was reconstituted as an elective body in 1933, consists of sixty members. The term of each member is twelve years and a quarter of the whole number of members retire every three years.[21] The vacancies then occurring are filled by an election, the electors being the members of the Legislative Council and the members of the Legislative Assembly voting as an electoral body according to a system of proportional representation, each voter having a transferable vote.[22]

[15]Inserted by Act No. 88 of 1954, s. 3.
[16]No. 91 of 1958, s. 3. The fault in the procedure lay in the fact that it would have no application if an Independent held the balance of power.
[17]Electoral Districts Act, 1971. Elections Act, 1915 (as amended), s. 9. C.A. Amendment Act, s. 21.
[18]C.A. Amendment Act No. 71 of 1975, s. 5, amending s. 18.
[19]C.A. Amendment Act, s. 18. Electoral Act, 1907, s. 17 (as amended). C.A. Amendment Act, s. 21.
[20]C.A. (N.S.W.), s. 10. C.A. (Vic.), s. 18. C.A. (Tas.), s. 12. C.A. (S.A.), s. 6. C.A. (W.A.), s. 3.
[21]C.A., ss. 17A, 17F (added by Act No. 2 of 1933).
[22]C.A., s. 17A (inserted by Act No. 2 of 1933, s. 3 (1)).

In Victoria the Legislative Council consists of forty-four members (twenty-two provinces returning two members each) elected by adult suffrage for a period of six years at periodical elections,[23] except in cases where a general election is held (which as we shall see later takes place in the event of a double dissolution) when one-half of the members elected hold their seats for three years only.[24]

The Legislative Council of South Australia consists of twenty-two members elected by adult suffrage according to a system of proportional representation (list system) with the State being one electorate for this purpose.[25] The members are elected for a period of six years at periodical elections. When the House of Assembly is dissolved or expires by effluxion of time, half the members of the Council who have completed their minimum terms retire and their vacancies are filled by election.[26]

In Tasmania the Legislative Council consists of nineteen members elected by adult suffrage for a period of six years. Periodical elections are held each year to fill the places of three members who retire, except that in every sixth year four members retire.[27]

The Western Australian Legislative Council consists of thirty members (fifteen provinces returning two members each, increased to thirty-two members with sixteen provinces returning two members each after 21 May 1977).[28] Each member holds his seat for six years.[29] Periodical elections are held every three years. Adult suffrage applies to these elections.[30]

RELATIONSHIP BETWEEN THE HOUSES

As has been pointed out, the Constitutions of the Australian States prohibit ordinary dissolutions of the Legislative Councils. However, in

[23] C.A., ss. 26, 27. These elections are held every three years, half the number of members retiring at this period. The increase in the members of the Council from a previous number of thirty-six to forty-four is to take place during the period 1976-79. See Electoral Provinces and Districts Act No. 8628 of 1974, s. 14.

[24] C.A., ss. 26, 27, 28. Electoral Provinces and Districts Act No. 8628 of 1974, s. 18(1).

[25] C.A., ss. 11, 19, 20, 20(a), (as amended by the Constitution and Electoral Acts Amendment Act No. 52 of 1973, ss. 5, 19). This increase (from a previous number of 20) is to take place over a period of two periodical elections.

[26] C.A., ss. 13, 14, 15 (as amended by the Constitution and Electoral Acts Amendment Act No. 5 of 1973, ss. 8, 9).

[27] C.A., s. 18 (amended by 9 & 10 Geo. VI, No. 48, s. 4), s. 19 (amended by 9 & 10 Geo. VI, No. 48, s. 5), s. 28 (amended by Constitution Act, No. 68 of 1968, s. 3).

[28] C.A. Amendment Act No. 71 of 1975, ss. 2, 3, amending ss. 5 and 6.

[29] C.A. Amendment Act, ss. 5, 6, 8 (as amended by C.A. Amendment Act, No. 2 of 1963).

[30] C.A. Amendment Act, s. 15 (amended by Act No. 72 of 1963).

the case of two States (Victoria and South Australia) provision is made for a dissolution of both Houses of Parliament when a deadlock occurs over a bill,[31] and in the case of one State (New South Wales) for the ultimate enactment of a bill, which is the subject of a deadlock, without the consent of the Legislative Council.[32] All the Constitutions recognize the primacy of the Lower House with respect to the initiation of money bills.[33]

New South Wales

S. 5 of the Constitution Act provides that any bill for appropriating revenue or for imposing any new tax shall originate in the Assembly. Detailed provisions for the resolution of deadlocks between the Houses are contained in ss. 5A and 5B.[34] The effect of s. 5A is to put the Legislative Council in a similar position to that which the House of Lords occupies in the British constitutional structure in relation to money bills of a certain category. Those bills which appropriate revenue for the ordinary annual services of the Government may be presented for the royal assent notwithstanding that the Council has rejected, failed to pass, or returned such bills to the Assembly. It is provided that the Legislative Council shall be deemed to have failed to pass such a bill if it is not returned to the Assembly within one month after its transmission to the Council. The consequence of this provision is that the Council cannot by inactivity frustrate the wishes of the Lower House in respect of an appropriation bill of this nature.[35] On the other hand, the Assembly cannot "tack on" or include provisions of an alien nature in an appropriation act. If it does, such provisions are deemed to be of no effect.[36]

With respect to all other types of bills passed by the Lower House, the opposition of the Upper House can only be overcome by a procedure which is laid down in s. 5B of the Act. This procedure consists of the following steps:

(1) The Legislative Council must reject, fail to pass, or pass with an amendment, a bill passed by the Assembly.

---

[31] C.A. (Vic.), s. 66. C.A. (S.A.), s. 41.
[32] C.A. (N.S.W.), ss. 5A and 5B.
[33] C.A. (N.S.W.), s. 5. C.A. (Vic.), s. 62. C.A. (S.A.), s. 61. C.A. (Tas.), s. 37. C.A. Amendment Act (W.A.), s. 46, as amended by Act No. 34, 1921, s. 2.
[34] These provisions were inserted by Act No. 2, 1933, s. 5.
[35] The Legislative Assembly may, of course, accept the amendment, in which case the bill will become law in the ordinary way.
[36] S. 5A (3).

(2) The bill must be passed again after an interval of three months by the Assembly and again rejected, not passed, or passed with an amendment by the Council.

(3) Provision is then made for the holding of a free conference of managers (a meeting of representatives of the Houses to discuss the bill).

(4) In the event of continued disagreement, a joint sitting of the members of both Houses may be convened by the Governor to discuss the bill.

(5) In the event of continued disagreement, the bill may be submitted to the electors of the State to be approved by a majority of them voting at a referendum.[37]

These provisions of the New South Wales Constitution Act were inserted by the Constitution (Legislative Council) Amendment Act[38] and were the culmination of a long history of disagreements between the Assembly and the Council which until 1933 consisted of members appointed by the Governor holding their seats for life.[39] It will be of value to briefly describe the crises which preceded the enactment of this amendment.[40] In 1925 a Labour ministry thwarted by a Council which it did not control requested the Governor to make twenty-five appointments to the Council. These appointments were in due course made by the Governor. Subsequently, the Government introduced a bill to abolish the Legislative Council but owing to the defection of several Labour members the bill was defeated. The Government then requested the Governor to make further appointments to the Council which would give it a definite majority. It may be noted that it was by this method, more popularly known as "swamping", that the Queensland Government in 1922 had secured the abolition of its Upper House.[41] However, in New South Wales the Governor refused

---

[37]The interpretation of the meaning of these provisions will be discussed later.
[38]Act No. 2, 1933.
[39]As prescribed by the original Constitution Act of 1855.
[40]See H. V. Evatt, *The King and His Dominion Governors,* with an Introduction by Zelman Cowen (2nd ed.; Melbourne: F. W. Cheshire, 1967), chaps. 14 and 19.
[41]*Ibid.,* pp.140-45. In 1917 a bill to abolish the Upper House had been submitted to a referendum but had been rejected. The referendum procedure had been laid down in the Parliamentary Bills Referendum Act (1908) as a means of overcoming deadlocks between Assembly and Council. in *Taylor v. Attorney-General for Queensland* (1916-17) 23 C.L.R. 457, the High Court upheld the validity of this legislation. However, the bill to abolish the council was rejected at the referendum. When in 1921, after the number of Legislative Councillors had been increased, the abolition bill was finally passed by both Houses, a petition was presented to the King requesting that he withhold assent to the bill but royal assent was given to it.

to make the additional appointments. The action of the Governor was subjected to criticism and attempts were made to influence the Secretary of State for the Dominions to direct the Governor to comply with the request of the ministry, but no action was taken by the United Kingdom Government.[42]

In 1929 the Labour Government was defeated and the new ministry led by Bavin passed an amendment to the Constitution Act designed to entrench provisions affecting the constitution of the Legislative Council.[43] The Constitution (Legislative Council) Amendment Act of 1929 introduced a new section, 7A. This section provided that no bill to abolish the Legislative Council should receive the royal assent unless it were passed by both Houses and approved by a majority of electors voting at a referendum. Subsequently, the Bavin ministry itself was defeated and the Lang ministry returned to power. It immediately set to work to undo the work of its predecessor by securing the passage through both Houses of a bill to abolish the Legislative Council. This bill was not submitted to a referendum as required by s. 7A (the 1929 amendment), the Government being of the opinion that this section could be repealed in the ordinary legislative manner. However, proceedings were taken by members of the Council to have the abolition bill declared invalid. In *Trethowan* v. *Attorney-General for New South Wales* both the High Court and the Privy Council decided that failure to follow the procedure laid down by s. 7A resulted in the invalidity of the abolition bill.[44] When the Lang ministry was dismissed by Sir Philip Game in 1932 the new ministry (led by Stevens) which came to power enacted amendments reconstituting the Legislative Council and providing machinery for the resolution of disagreements between the two Houses.[45] It was at this stage that ss. 5A and 5B referred to above were inserted in the Constitution Act. It is important to note that sub-section 5 of s. 5B provided that the deadlock machinery was to apply to bills abolishing the Council, thus furnishing a method of abolishing the Council inconsistent with s. 7A which re-

---

[42] The negotiations in London on behalf of the Government were conducted by Mr. McTiernan, at that time Attorney-General of New South Wales (now a Justice of the High Court).
[43] Act No. 29, 1929.
[44] (1930-31) 44 C.L.R. 394 (High Court); [1932] A.C. 526 (Privy Council).
[45] Act No. 2, 1933. This Act was passed by both Houses and approved by a majority of electors voting at a referendum. In *Piddington* v. *Attorney-General for New South Wales* (1933) 33 S.R. (N.S.W.) 317 and *Doyle* v. *Attorney-General for New South Wales* (1933) 33 S.R. (N.S.W.) 484, the validity of this legislation was upheld by the New South Wales Full Court.

quired passage of an abolition bill by *both* Houses before submission to a referendum. As has been pointed out, the effect of s. 5B was to prescribe a complex procedure whereby a disagreement between the Houses could be resolved—a procedure which in effect substituted the electors for the Upper House at the final stage in the deadlock procedure.

In 1959 the New South Wales legislature decided to make use of these deadlock provisions to abolish the Legislative Council and its action at that time led to a case of great constitutional significance. In that year the New South Wales Government brought in the Constitution Amendment (Legislative Council Abolition) Bill. This bill provided by s. 2 that the Legislative Council was thereby abolished. A new section was added to the Constitution Act by inserting s. 7B after s. 7A. S. 7B provided that a Legislative Council should not be re-established except in the manner provided by the section, which was submission to a referendum and approval by the electors. The bill was passed by the Assembly but returned to it by the Council without consideration on the ground that it should have originated in the Council. It was again passed by the Assembly and again returned without consideration thereon by the Council. A request for a free conference as provided for in s. 5B was made by the Assembly but this was rejected by the Council. The Governor then convened a joint sitting of members of both Houses. At this sitting[46] deliberation on the bill took place. Subsequently, the Assembly directed that the bill be submitted to a referendum. At this stage, the plaintiffs, the majority of whom were members of the Council, commenced proceedings seeking a declaration that the bill could not properly be submitted to a referendum and an injunction restraining the defendants, who were ministers of the Crown and the Electoral Commissioner, from submitting the bill to a referendum. The suit was dismissed by the New South Wales Full Court[47] and its decision was upheld by the High Court.[48]

One argument brought forward by the plaintiffs was that the Council in returning the bill to the Assembly without deliberation had not

---

[46]The Council had passed a motion in the meantime to the effect that it did not consider that a situation had arisen for holding the joint sitting and resolved that its members should not participate. However, a number of Legislative Councillors attended the joint sitting.

[47]The judgment of the New South Wales Full Court is reported in 77 W.N. (N.S.W.) 767.

[48]*Clayton* v. *Heffron* (1960-61) 105 C.L.R. 214. The majority decision was delivered by Dixon, C. J., McTiernan, Taylor and Windeyer, JJ. See comment in 4 *University of Queensland Law Journal* (1961), 23.

rejected or failed to pass the bill. It was argued that the words used in s. 5B envisaged deliberation on the bill which was subject to a deadlock and did not extend to a case where the bill was returned *in limine* on the ground of privilege. But the High Court was of the opinion that s. 5B applied both to active consideration of a bill by the Upper House and passive conduct on its part as in this case.[49]

It was argued, secondly, that the requirement as to a free conference between managers of the Houses was mandatory[50] and that failure to comply with the procedure laid down had led to nullity in the subsequent steps taken by the Assembly. On this point, the majority of the High Court considered that the provision in question was merely directory and that the failure to abide by it did not invalidate the subsequent steps taken to resolve the deadlock. It was pointed out that the power involved was a power to pass a public general statute and that, if non-compliance with the requirement of a free conference or a joint sitting invalidated the act, subsequent statutes enacted by the new legislature brought into being under the amendment would have no force. An interpretation which avoided such great public inconvenience was therefore to be preferred.[51]

It is clear, therefore, that the New South Wales Legislative Council cannot prevent a bill which is the subject of deadlock between the two Houses from being submitted to a referendum by refusing to participate in the procedure laid down by s. 5B, and that any bill (other than those covered by s. 5A), including a bill to abolish the Council itself, may become law after passage through the Assembly and approval by the electorate, provided that the Assembly shows itself willing to participate with the Council in the conciliation procedures prescribed.[52]

---

[49] 105 C.L.R., at pp. 242-43.

[50] The distinction between a mandatory and a directory provision in a statute is described by P. B. Maxwell, *The Interpretation of Statutes* (10th ed.; London: Sweet & Maxwell, 1953), p.375, in the following manner: "The reports are full of cases dealing with statutory provisions which are devoid of indication of intention regarding the effect of non-compliance with them. In some of them, the conditions, form and other attendant circumstances prescribed by the statute have been regarded as essential to the act or thing regulated by it and their omission has been held fatal to its validity. In others, such prescriptions have been considered as merely directory, the neglect of which did not affect its validity or involve any other consequence than a liability to a penalty, if any were proposed, for breach of the enactment."

[51] 105 C.L.R., at pp. 246-48.

[52] It was at the referendum stage that the Constitution Amendment (Legislative Council Abolition) Bill came to grief: it was rejected by a majority of the electors.

Victoria

Victorian constitutional history too has been marked by disagreements between the Lower and Upper Houses.[53] In Victoria, however, the provisions relating to the position of the Legislative Assembly and Council in relation to money bills and to the procedure to be followed in the event of disagreement between the Houses are different from those in New South Wales. In the first place, the Victorian Constitution does not invest the Assembly with complete supremacy in the matter of money bills; in the second place, there is no provision corresponding to s. 5B of the New South Wales Act. However, the Victorian Constitution does make provision for a dissolution of both Houses in the event of a deadlock, if certain conditions are fulfilled.[54]

With respect to money bills it is provided that all appropriation bills and taxation bills shall originate in the Assembly and may be rejected but not altered by the Council.[55] However, the force of this provision is weakened by another which allows the Council to suggest amendments to a bill at certain stages in its passage through that House.[56] It is further provided that an annual appropriation bill shall deal only with appropriation.[57] This provision, designed to prevent "tacking" of alien provisions to an appropriation bill, does not state the effect which will follow if such "tacking" occurs. It will be recalled that the similar New South Wales provision denies legal effect to the alien clause. It is submitted that the Victorian Legislative Council would be able to amend that part of an appropriation bill which dealt with alien matter. If, however, a bill containing alien subject matter was passed into law without objection by the Council, the whole act would stand; in other words, the section in question would be treated as a directory provision designed to prevent the Assembly from using the machinery of s. 62 for an improper purpose. If the Legislative Council did not take advantage of its power to reject the whole bill or amend the alien provision in it, then the purpose of the section would be fulfilled and the validity of the bill could not be questioned after it had received the

---

[53] For an analysis of the history of the Victorian Constitution and the relationship between the Houses see Z. Cowen, "A Historical Survey of the Victorian Constitution 1856-1956", 1 *Melbourne University Law Review* (1957-58), 9, especially pp. 36 *et seq.* A. B. Keith, *Responsible Government in the Dominions* (2nd ed.; Oxford: Clarendon Press, 1928), I, 474 *et seq.*
[54] C.A., s. 66.
[55] C.A., s. 62.
[56] C.A., s. 64 (2).
[57] C.A., s. 65.

royal assent.[58]

S. 66 of the Constitution Act Amendment Act makes provision for the resolution of deadlocks. The procedure consists of two stages: a "staggered" double dissolution and a joint sitting of both Houses. It is to be noted that these deadlock provisions apply to all bills (including appropriation bills) except those providing for the abolition of the Council or amending the provisions of the Constitution (ss. 66, 67, 68) relating to the resolution of deadlocks.[59] The steps to be followed in resolving a deadlock between the Houses over a particular bill are as follows:

(1) The bill is passed by the Assembly and rejected[60] by the Council.

(2) The Assembly is dissolved by the Governor (not later than six months before its normal expiry time) by a proclamation specifying that the dissolution is granted only because of the disagreement of the Houses in respect of the bill.

(3) The bill is passed by the new Assembly in the next session after the elapse of a certain time interval and is again rejected by the Council.

(4) In this event, the Governor may dissolve the Legislative Council (but not within one month after the Bill is last rejected or within nine months after any general or periodical election for the Council).

(5) If after such a dissolution the bill is again passed by the Assembly and rejected by the Council, the Governor may convene a joint sitting of the members of both Houses. At such a joint sitting the bill (with or without amendments made at the joint sitting) will be deemed to have been duly passed by the Council and the Assembly if it is carried by an absolute majority of the whole number of members of the Council and Assembly.[61]

The Victorian provisions, as can be seen, provide a more complex

---

[58]See *Osborn* v. *The Commonwealth of Australia* (1911) 12 C.L.R. 321, at pp. 336-37, per Griffith, C.J. This view is strengthened by the fact that s. 65 refers to "bills" not to "laws".

[59]C.A., s. 68 (5).

[60]C.A., s. 68 defines the circumstances under which a bill is considered to have been rejected by the Council. Rejection is deemed to have taken place when the bill is not passed within two months of its being transmitted to the Council, or where the second and third readings are not, within two months after it has been so transmitted, passed with the concurrence of an absolute majority of the whole number of the members of the Council without amendment or with such amendments only as may be agreed to by both Houses.

[61]C.A., ss. 66, 67.

procedure than is the case with the New South Wales provisions and one which is more favourable to the Legislative Council. The dissolution and the joint sitting replace the New South Wales referendum; in other words, in the case of Victoria the electors can only indirectly pass judgment on the bill which is the cause of the disagreement while in New South Wales they can directly determine the fate of the bill which is submitted to them at the referendum. While the threat of their dissolution may in Victoria induce the Council to accept a bill passed by a newly elected Assembly following dissolution of the old Assembly, an obstinate Council may continue to withhold its assent to the bill. And when, after a dissolution of the Council, the bill is finally presented to a joint sitting of the members of both Houses,[62] it must secure an absolute majority of the whole number of members of the Assembly and Council. Even at this stage the Council has the legal power (although weakened) to affect the outcome of the bill.

South Australia

The South Australian Constitution provides that money bills (including money clauses) shall originate in the House of Assembly.[63] Money bills are defined to cover appropriation, taxation and loan bills, excluding bills providing funds for the purposes of local authorities or bills imposing fines, penalties, or fees for licences and services.[64] The Legislative Council cannot amend money bills or clauses but may return to the Assembly such bills or clauses with suggestions for amendments except where the bill is an appropriation bill appropriating money for a previously authorized purpose.[65] It is provided that appropriation bills of this nature shall not contain provisions appropriating money for any purpose other than a previously authorized one.[66] The Act says nothing as to the right of the Legislative Council to reject a money bill—it only refers to the amending of such bills—and on ordinary principles of statutory interpretation the power of rejection must still be regarded as vested in

---

[62] It seems clear that the requirement of a joint sitting is mandatory for it is part of the process by which the bill becomes law. The position may be contrasted with the joint sitting provided for in the New South Wales Constitution which is merely a forum for arriving at agreement by discussion and not an occasion when the bill itself is to be approved by members voting as a component part of the legislature.

[63] C.A., s. 61.

[64] C.A., s. 60.

[65] C.A., s. 62. A "previously authorized" purpose is a purpose authorized by previous act or decision of the House.

[66] C.A., s. 63.

the Council.[67] It is also clear that the sections relating to the content of money bills are directory rather than mandatory for it is expressly provided that any infringement of these provisions shall not affect the validity of any Act assented to by the Governor.[68]

The South Australian Constitution does not contain any provision for the resolution of deadlocks in the manner laid down in the New South Wales Constitution. It does however provide for a double dissolution and a change in the composition of the Council when certain conditions are fulfilled.[69] These conditions are as follows:

(1) Passage of a bill through the Assembly and rejection (or failure to pass) by the Council.

(2) A dissolution of the Assembly and a general election for that House.

(3) Subsequent passage of the bill (or a similar bill) through the Assembly with an absolute majority of the whole number of members of the Assembly at the second and third readings.

(4) Rejection of the bill (or failure to pass) by the Council.

When such conditions are fulfilled "it shall be lawful but not obligatory upon the Governor" within six months after the last rejection or failure to pass to dissolve both Houses or to issue writs for the election of two additional members for the Council.[70]

It is clear therefore that the only method of ultimately overcoming the opposition of the Legislative Council to a bill passed by the House of Assembly is for the Government to secure a majority in the Council through the election of additional members favourable to the passage of the bill. There is no procedure similar to the Victorian procedure whereby, after the dissolution, the bill may be submitted to a joint sitting of both Houses.[71]

---

[67] According to the maxim *expressio unius est exclusio alterius.*

[68] C.A., s. 64.

[69] C.A., s. 41.

[70] C.A., s. 41 (as amended by the Constitution and Electoral Acts Amendment Act No. 52 of 1973, s. 14.) However, vacancies occurring in the new Council after the election are not filled except to bring the representation in the Council up to its normal number.

[71] The nature of the relationship between the Lower and Upper Houses was the subject of a long debate in the South Australian Legislative Assembly in 1857. See *Proceedings of the Parliament of South Australia* 1857-58, Vol. II, No. 101.

Tasmania

There have been a number of disagreements between the two Houses in Tasmania.[72] The Tasmanian Constitution provides that revenue or money bills, apart from those imposing penalties, fines, or fees for services, shall originate in the House of Assembly.[73] Appropriation bills must not contain alien matter or authorize appropriation for a period longer than one year.[74] If a provision in an appropriation bill infringes these conditions it is void.[75] The Council cannot amend appropriation, income tax, or land tax bills although it may request amendments to them.[76] It may amend any other bill provided that it does not insert in such bills any provision for the appropriation of money or for increasing any burden on the people.[77] It is expressly provided that the Council may reject any bill.[78] In all cases not expressly provided for by the Act, the Assembly and Council have equal power.[79] There is no provision in the Tasmanian Constitution for resolving any deadlock or disagreement between the Houses.

Western Australia

Section 46 of the Western Australian Constitution Acts Amendment Act[80] requires money bills to originate in the Legislative Assembly. Bills appropriating money for the ordinary annual services of government must deal only with that subject matter while taxation bills must deal only with the imposition of taxation. The Legislative Council cannot amend bills appropriating money for the ordinary an-

---

[72] See A. B. Keith, *The Dominions as Sovereign States* (London: Macmillan & Co., 1938), pp.229-30. In 1924 the Acting Governor assented to an Appropriation Bill which had been passed by the Lower House but not by the Upper House which had inserted an amendment in the bill. In the following year the Governor assented to a Land and Income Tax Bill from which the Upper House had deleted a clause. These assents can only be regarded as unconstitutional in view of the fact that at this stage there was no provision in the Constitution Act which prohibited the Upper House from amending such bills. However, no legal action was taken to test the validity of the acts. In 1926 the Tasmanian legislature amended the Constitution Act so as, *inter alia*, to prohibit the Council from amending these types of bills. The provision in question is s. 42 of the Constitution Act. See, further, Keith, *Responsible Government in the Dominions*, II, 1246-47.

[73] S. 37 (as amended in 1967).
[74] S. 39.
[75] S. 40.
[76] S. 42 (1).
[77] S. 42 (2).
[78] S. 44.
[79] S. 45.
[80] Inserted by Act No. 34 of 1921.

nual services of government, taxation bills or loan bills or any other bill in such a way as to increase any proposed charge or burden on the people. However, it may return such bills requesting amendments (providing they do not increase any burden on the people). In all other cases the Legislative Council is given equal power with the Legislative Assembly.[81] There is no provision for the resolution of deadlocks.

PRIVILEGES OF THE HOUSES

At common law, Houses of colonial Parliaments possessed powers and privileges which were necessary for their self-protection and the proper discharge of their legislative functions.[82] Without legislative authorization, these Houses could not exercise the full privileges attaching to the House of Commons which were derived from the *lex et consuetudo Parliamenti*. In the case of the Australian legislatures, the original Constitution Acts fell into two categories. Power was conferred on the Victorian, South Australian, and Western Australian Parliaments to define the privileges of these Houses, the proviso being that the privileges thus defined should not exceed those of the House of Commons.[83] Pursuant to this conferment of power, these Parliaments have adopted the privileges of the House of Commons.[84] In the other three States, the full powers of the House of Commons were not adopted but statutory definitions of particular privileges have been made. In these latter States, therefore, the extent and nature of parliamentary privilege has its source in the older common law and specific legislative enactments. It seems however that these States could add to their privileges so as to make them as complete as those of the House of Commons.[85]

One of the most important privileges residing in the Houses of State Parliaments is that which protects freedom of speech. While it is clear

---

[81] C.A. Amendment Act, s. 46 (5).
[82] *Kielly* v. *Carson* (1842) 4 Moo. P.C.C. 63. See Enid Campbell, *Parliamentary Privilege in Australia* (Melbourne: Melbourne University Press, 1966), chap. 1.
[83] 18 & 19 Vict., c.55, s. 35 (Victoria). 53 & 54 Vict., c.26, s. 36 (Western Australia). Act No. 2, 1855-56, s. 35 (South Australia).
[84] C. A. (Vict.), s. 19. C.A. (S.A.), s. 38. Parliamentary Privileges Act (W.A.), 1891, s. 1.
[85] Campbell, *Parliamentary Privilege in Australia,* p.12. In *Armstrong* v. *Budd* [1969] 1 N.S.W.R. 649, it was decided that a House of the New South Wales Parliament had the power to expel a member if such action was necessary to protect the orderly exercise of the legislative function. The Courts could determine whether the power to expel existed, but it was for the House to determine whether a proper case had arisen for the exercise of the power subject only to the Court's review of any excessive exercise of the power.

that this privilege protects the members of the Houses from defamation actions brought in respect of utterances in the House and just as clear that it does not extend to defamatory publications not related to parliamentary duties which are made outside the House, there are certain areas lying between to which some uncertainty attaches, e.g. the right of a royal commissioner to require the attendance of members to answer questions relating to facts which were the subject of statements made in the House.[86]

---

[86] *Ibid.*, chap. 2, especially pp.38-42.

CHAPTER FOUR

The Relationship Between the Legislature and the Executive

IN THE FIRST PART of this work we examined the development of the doctrine of responsible government in the Constitutions of the Australian colonies.[1] Although the various Constitution Acts in some form or other gave recognition to this doctrine, its operation in the Australian States is to be derived from convention and practice as well as from formal law. The doctrine itself is characterized by two features:

(1) That the Executive is subject to control by Parliament and holds office by the sanction of Parliament.

(2) That the powers vested in the Governor by the various Constitution Acts are, with certain exceptions, not exercisable by him personally but on the advice of and through the ministers responsible to Parliament.[2]

It is clear that it was not until the enactment and coming into force of the Constitution Acts in 1855-56 that this doctrine became part of Australian constitutional law. In the first seventy years of Australian constitutional development the Executive was not subject to parliamentary control. The officers of government were appointed by the Governor and the Secretary of State for the Colonies, and their executive status was therefore subordinate to and subject to the jurisdiction of those officials. It is true that the ministers invariably held seats in the legislative bodies as official nominees, but, while this made them subject to legislative criticism, it did not make them subject to legislative control.[3] Moreover, the Governors participated in the ad-

---

[1] *Supra*, chaps. 1 and 2.
[2] The second aspect of this doctrine is often referred to as the doctrine of ministerial responsibility.
[3] "The legislature might oppose the policy of the officials as much as it pleased, but it could not force them to resign, and the constituencies had no chance of expressing their opinions; for the seats of the officials were nominee, not elective, and a dissolution, while it might not strengthen the Government, could not defeat it. Practically speaking, an official could only be dismissed for personal misbehaviour or incapacity, and the Governor's dismissal of him was always liable to review by the Home authorities." E. Jenks, *The Government of Victoria* (London: Macmillan & Co., 1891), p.209.

ministration of the affairs of the colonies and were not mere figureheads through which executive action was confirmed.[4]

The changes brought about by the new Constitution Acts of 1855-56, supplemented by the conventions[5] which were presupposed by those Acts, were of major importance. From that date in all the existing colonies except Western Australia, it was recognized that the members of a ministry could not hold office without the support of Parliament, that they were liable to retire if they did not gain or retain this support and that the only effective way of obtaining this support was by securing a seat in Parliament.[6] A vote adverse to the Government on a critical issue in the Lower House, the popularly elected House, would indicate that the Government did not have the support of the House and ought therefore to resign. In the second place it was recognized that the Governor would ordinarily exercise the powers vested in him by the Constitution Act or Royal Instructions through his ministers although, insofar as he still retained powers in matters of Imperial rather than of local concern, he could in such cases act without this advice as an officer of the Imperial Government.[7] There was some dispute over the nature of these powers but it was agreed that the power of reserving bills for the royal assent was included within this category.[8] Apart from such cases it was also agreed that in cases of constitutional importance where there was doubt as to whether the ministry had the support of Parliament the Governor might exercise certain powers on his own initiative. This field of power where he could act against advice of the ministry was known as the reserve power.[9] Finally, there were some matters[10] which because of

[4]A. C. V. Melbourne, *Early Constitutional Development in Australia: New South Wales* 1788-1856, *Queensland* 1859-1922, ed. R. B. Joyce (2nd ed.; St. Lucia: University of Queensland Press, 1963), *passim.*

[5]"Much therefore that is at the very root of the constitutions of our self-governing colonies is unwritten, though it is none the less constitutional because its origin lies in a practice which is nowhere formally recorded, and which develops new rules in the course of years." H. Jenkyns, *British Rule and Jurisdiction Beyond the Seas* (Oxford: Clarendon Press, 1902), p.59.

[6]E. Jenks, *The Government of Victoria*, p.271; W. I. Jennings, *Cabinet Government* (3rd ed.; Cambridge: Cambridge University Press, 1959), p.340.

[7]A. B. Keith, *Responsible Government in the Dominions* (2nd ed.; Oxford: Clarendon Press, 1928), I, 209 *et seq.*

[8]*Ibid.*, p.211. For a list of reserved bills which were not assented to by the monarch and bills which were disallowed see J. Quick and R. R. Garran, *The Annotated Constitution of the Australian Commonwealth* (Sydney: Angus & Robertson, 1901), pp.695-97.

[9]H. V. Evatt, *The King and His Dominion Governors*, with an Introduction by Zelman Cowen (2nd ed.; Melbourne: F. W. Cheshire, 1967), pp.15-29.

[10]For example, the prerogative of honours. See Keith, *Responsible Government in the Dominions*, pp.85 *et seq.*

their Imperial nature were outside the powers of the Governor and vested in the monarch alone.

Not all, however, accepted this analysis of the relationship between the executive and the legislature after 1855-56. Sir George Higinbotham, a leading Victorian lawyer and politician, who was afterwards to become Chief Justice of Victoria, considered that Victoria derived from its Constitution Act a complete doctrine of responsible government (except in matters of Imperial concern).[11] He put forward his views forcibly both as a member of the Victorian legislature and on the Supreme Court Bench. The *locus classicus* of his analysis of the doctrine of responsible government is to be found in the case of *Toy* v. *Musgrove*.[12] In this case the issue was whether the Collector of Customs for Victoria, acting on orders from a minister of the Crown, could prevent aliens from entering the colony.[13] Insofar as there was no statute *directly* authorizing exclusion, reliance was placed on the prerogative right of the Crown to effect such exclusion. This issue in turn depended on whether the Victorian Executive could be regarded as invested with the prerogatives of the Crown insofar as they were necessary to further the order and good government of the colony.

The majority of the judges were of the opinion that the Victorian Constitution Act had not introduced a complete system of responsible government, and, insofar as there was no mention in the Victorian Constitution Act or in the Royal Instructions of the grant to the Governor of the prerogative right to exclude aliens, that the exclusion was not justified by law.[14] However, Higinbotham, C. J., and Kerferd, J., took the view that complete responsible government had been introduced by the Constitution Act and that the prerogative right in question which was exercised for the order and good government of Victoria was necessarily vested in the Executive.[15] Higinbotham, C. J., put forward a number of propositions which may be summarized as follows:

(1) The Constitution Act was the sole source of the constitutional rights of self-government of the people of Victoria.

---

[11] For a discussion of his views see E. E. Morris, *Memoir of George Higinbotham* (London: Macmillan & Co., 1895), chap. 18. S. Encel, *Cabinet Government in Australia* (Melbourne: Melbourne University Press, 1962), p.24.

[12] (1888) 14 V.L.R. 349.

[13] The plaintiff was a Chinese who had arrived as an immigrant in Melbourne on an English ship.

[14] 14 V.L.R., at pp.413-23 (Williams, J.); 423-34 (Holroyd, J.); 434-35 (A'Beckett, J.); 435-43 (Wrenfordsley, J.).

[15] *Ibid.*, at pp.371-98, 398-413.

(2) The doctrine of responsible government had found "adequate though obscure" expression in this Act.

(3) The Victorian Legislature and Executive had been invested with functions similar to those possessed by the Parliament and Government of Great Britain in relation to the internal affairs of Victoria.

(4) The ministers of the Crown were responsible for the exercise of the powers of the Governor and they alone had the right to control him in the exercise of these powers.

(5) This executive power so far as it was consistent with statute law and treaties might be exercised in such a way as to perform all acts necessary for the government of the colony.[16]

The conclusion which Higinbotham, C.J., reached from these propositions was that the Victorian Executive had a right to exclude aliens.[17] The contrary view to that of Higinbotham, C.J., can be succinctly summed up in the words of Williams, J., one of the majority judges, that Victoria had "merely an instalment of self-government".[18] When the case went on appeal to the Privy Council the substantial issue upon which the case went off in the Supreme Court was not discussed and the matter was decided in favour of the Victorian Government on other grounds.[19]

There is no doubt that in the nineteenth century the Imperial Government itself did not accept the proposition that complete responsible government had been attained by the Australian colonies. It was recognized in various dispatches from the Colonial Secretary that the Governor had the right to refuse the advice of his ministers in matters of local concern in exceptional circumstances and in fact a number of colonial Governors acted contrary to advice given to them by ministers.[20] The view of Keith,[21] Jenks,[22] and Windeyer[23] that responsible government was not introduced solely by the Constitution Acts, in one fell swoop as it were, seems to be more in keeping with constitutional practice in the Australian colonies in the nineteenth century than does the view of Higinbotham. While one can agree with the latter that the doctrine was implicitly recognized in the Constitution

---

[16] *Ibid.*, at pp.396-97.
[17] *Ibid.*, at pp.397-98.
[18] *Ibid.*, at p.416.
[19] [1891] A.C. 272. The main ground was that an alien had no right enforceable by action to enter British territory.
[20] See examples in Keith, *Responsible Government in the Dominions*, I, 122 *et seq.*
[21] *Ibid.*, p.117.
[22] *The Government of Victoria*, p.207.
[23] "Responsible Government", 42 *Royal Australian Historical Society Journal* (1957), p.271.

Acts, one cannot agree that it was solely dependent on this source—it depended also on the attitudes and practices of the Imperial Government and Governors which accompanied the grant of self-government and on a gradual development of an awareness—an *opinio iuris*—that the Governor must act on the advice of his ministers.[24] Even today as we shall see there are circumstances which would seem to justify the exercise by the Governor of his executive powers contrary to the advice of his ministers.

RESPONSIBLE GOVERNMENT IN THE CONSTITUTION ACTS

The doctrine of responsible government is recognized in all the Constitution Acts of the States, in some to a greater extent than in others. It is recognized implicitly in those provisions which vest the appointment of officers liable to retire on political grounds in the Governor. Such provisions are to be found in the New South Wales, Victorian, Queensland and Western Australian Acts.[25] In the South Australian Act the terminology is different: in that State the power is vested in the Governor to appoint *and* dismiss those officers who are required to be members of Parliament.[26] The South Australian Act is the only one which expressly vests in the Governor power of dismissal as well as of appointment but convention would support the exercise of the power of dismissal of ministers from office in extreme cases in other States. There is no provision in the Tasmanian Act corresponding to any of the provisions in the other Acts. In that State, the doctrine is based on convention alone.[27] It is also recognized in the various acts that acceptance of ministerial office does not involve resignation from or the vacating of a seat in Parliament which is the result of an acceptance of an office of profit under the Crown.[28] The Victorian and South Australian Acts go further than the other Acts in that they make it obligatory for a minister to secure a seat in Parliament within three months of appointment to ministerial office,[29] but this would today be

---

[24] K. Bailey, "Self-Government in Australia 1860-1900", *Cambridge History of the British Empire* (Cambridge: Cambridge University Press, 1929), VII, 397.

[25] C.A. (N.S.W.), s. 47. C.A. (Vic.), s. 88. C.A. (Qld.), s. 14.

[26] C.A., s. 68.

[27] R. Anderson, "The Constitutional Framework", in *The Government of the Australian States*, ed. S. R. Davis (Melbourne: Longmans, 1960), p.11.

[28] C.A. (N.S.W.), ss. 17B(3), 26, and 27. C.A. (Vic.), s. 53. C.A. (S.A.), s. 45. C.A. (Tas.), s. 32. Queensland Officials in Parliament Act, 1896 (as amended), ss. 3, 5. C.A. Amendment Act (W.A.), s. 37.

[29] C.A. (Vic.), s. 51. C.A. (S.A.), s. 66.

required by convention in the other States. The number of ministerial officers is provided for by statute and in some cases a specified proportion must be selected from a particular House.[30]

The most important weapon which Parliament holds vis-a-vis the Executive, and which can be used to bring about the resignation of a ministry which no longer has the support of the House, is its control over the expenditure of public moneys. The principle of parliamentary control which is fundamental to the British Constitution[31] is part of the constitutional law of the Australian States. Provision is made in the Constitution Acts of four of the States for a Consolidated Revenue Fund into which state revenue is paid. Appropriations or disbursements from these Funds may be effected only under the authority of statute.[32] In Tasmania and South Australia the principle of parliamentary control is recognized by a combination of convention and statutory provisions (outside the Constitution Acts).[33]

The principle has received judicial examination in *Australian Alliance Insurance Co.* v. *Goodwyn*[34] decided by the Queensland Full Court. In that case one of the questions to be determined was whether the Government could by Order in Council make provision for the disbursement of money from consolidated revenue to a government insurance office. The members of the Court were of the opinion that the Order in Council was invalid in that it lacked statutory support and was in fact contrary to s. 39 of the Queensland Constitution Act.[35] It

---

[30] In New South Wales provision is made for eighteen ministers (C.A., 2nd Schedule as amended by the Parliamentary Allowances and Salaries Act). Provision is also made by the Constitution and Other Acts (Amendment) No. 67 of 1975, Part IVA for parliamentary secretaries, to be appointed by the Premier. In Victoria of seventeen ordinary ministers, not more than thirteen at any one time shall be members of the Assembly and not more than five shall be members of the Council (C.A., s. 50). In South Australia there are twelve ministers (C.A., s. 65 (1)). In Tasmania there are ten ministers of whom nine are to be chosen from the House of Assembly (Ministers of the Crown Act, 1923 as amended). Queensland has eighteen ministers (Officials in Parliament Act as amended, s. 3(1)). In Western Australia there are thirteen ministers. At least one of these must be a member of the Legislative Council (C.A. Amendment Act, s. 43).

[31] See Keith, *Responsible Government in the Dominions*, I, 361 *et seq.*

[32] C.A. (N.S.W.), ss. 39, 45. (C.A. Vic.), ss. 89, 92. C.A. (Qld.), ss. 34, 39. C.A. (W.A.), ss. 64, 72. In *State of New South Wales* v. *Bardolph* (1935) 52 C.L.R. 455 it was held that the absence of parliamentary appropriation did not affect the validity of contracts entered into by ministers under which an obligation to pay moneys arose. But such contracts could not be enforced before such appropriation was made.

[33] See Anderson, "The Constitutional Framework", p.16.

[34] (1916) St. R. Qd. 255. See also *Alcock* v. *Fergie* (1867) 4 W.W. & A'B. (L.) 285. A recent example of the application of the principle is *Re Bonner* [1963] Qd. R. 488, where the Supreme Court of Queensland held that casual revenue accruing to the Crown could not be dealt with by ministerial direction but was subject to the appropriation provisions of the Queensland Constitution.

[35] The section which required appropriation to be by act of Parliament.

was true, the Court said, that on occasions revenue had been appropriated without parliamentary sanction in cases of extreme public emergency. However, such necessity did not entail validity:

We cannot see that the occasional or frequent breach or violation of the law in any way affects the question, even if such breach is counselled on an occasion of supreme public emergency as justifiable or excusable in the loose sense in which those words are used. The fact remains that all such actions are breaches of the law, and in a proper case arising properly before us, it seems to us not only our right but our duty to make the declaration as to their legality.[36]

The emergency situation can be dealt with by special machinery in finance and audit acts. In fact there are provisions in State statute law which provide for the disbursement of moneys from consolidated revenue in cases of emergency which cannot be foreseen when the ordinary appropriation acts are passed.[37]

THE POSITION OF THE GOVERNOR AND MINISTERIAL RESPONSIBILITY

The Governors of the Australian States are appointed by the Queen during her pleasure under Letters Patent constituting the office of Governor.[38] This latter instrument is accompanied by Royal Instructions under the Sign Manual and Signet.[39] From these sources are

[36](1916) St. R. Qd., at p.255.
[37]See Anderson, "The Constitutional Framework", p.16. In *Goodwyn's Case* the Full Court at pp.250-51 expressed the opinion that the provisions of the Constitution Act controlling disbursement of public moneys were inflexible and could not be modified by later statutes unless these later statues expressly repealed them. This view as to the inflexibility of State constitutions which had been adopted by the earlier case of *Cooper* v. *Commissioner of Income Tax* (1907) 4 C.L.R. 1304 was rejected by the Privy Council in *McCawley* v. *The King* [1920] A.C. 691. The postscript to *Goodwyn's Case* was that subsequently the Queensland legislature made provision for the disbursement of moneys for the contemplated purpose by an enabling statute.
[38]The appointment is recommended to the Queen by the State Government through the Foreign and Commonwealth Office on whose formal advice the Queen would act. The wishes of the State Government on the appointment would be accepted by the British Government although in the past this has not been so. See Anderson, "The Constitutional Framework", p.14. The term for which a State Governor holds his appointment is normally five years but this may be extended. Dormant commissions which operate on the death or absence of the Governor confer on the Administrator or Lieutenant-Governor (who is usually the Chief Justice of the State) power to exercise the functions of Governor.
[39]The power to issue Instructions is given by the Australian Constitutions Act (1842), s. 40. The Instructions are substantially the same for all State Governors. The Queensland Instructions are set out in *Acts and Laws Relating to the Constitution of the State of Queensland* (Brisbane: Government Printer, 1951), pp.19-21. See D. B. Swinfen, "The Legal Status of Royal Instructions to Colonial Governors", (1968) *Juridical Review* 21; Enid Campbell, "Crown Lands Grants: Form and Validity", 40 *Australian Law Journal* (1966) 35 at pp.36-38.

derived the formal powers of the Governor. Under these instruments, an Executive Council[40] is set up to advise the Governor in the exercise of his powers and rules are laid down as to the classes of bills which must be reserved for the royal assent. Clause VI of these Instructions is of interest. It reads:

> In the execution of the powers and authorities vested in him the Governor shall be guided by the advice of the Excutive Council, but if in any case he shall see sufficient cause to dissent from the opinion of the said Council he may act in the exercise of his said powers and authorities in opposition to the opinion of the Council, reporting the matter to Us without delay, with the reasons for his so acting.

The status of these instructions will be referred to later, but at this stage it may be pointed out that Clause VI does not seem to recognize fully the principle of ministerial responsibility.

The members of the Executive Council are appointed by the Governor. No formal rules are laid down by State laws as to the composition of the Executive Council except in Victoria and South Australia where it is provided that the responsible officers of Government shall ex officio be members of the Executive Council.[41] In the other States the Executive Council consists of ministers of the Crown by convention.[42] As far as retirement is concerned, the convention in New South Wales, South Australia, and Western Australia is for a member to resign on ceasing to hold a ministerial post. In Victoria, Queensland and Tasmania a minister continues to be a member of the Council even after he ceases to hold a ministerial post but the practice is to summon to the Council only those who are ministers for the time being.[43]

The primary function of the Governor is to assent to bills passed by the legislature.[44] In four of the States, New South Wales, Victoria, Queensland, and Western Australia, the assent is given in the Queen's name;[45] in South Australia and Tasmania in the Governor's name.[46] Certain classes of bills must be reserved for the royal assent under the

[40]The quorum is the President (who will usually be the Governor) and two Councillors.

[41]C.A. (Vic.), s. 50 (2). C.A. (S.A.), s. 66 (2).

[42]Anderson, "The Constitutional Framework", p.10.

[43]*Ibid.*

[44]Australian Constitutions Act (1842), s. 31. Under s. 32 of this Act the monarch may disallow a bill assented to by the Governor. However, it seems that, if an occasion for the exercise of this power arose today, it would be exercised on the advice of the ministers of the State in which the law was enacted (forwarded through the Foreign and Commonwealth Office). See n. 48.

[45]C.A. (N.S.W.), s. 3 C.A. (Vic.), s. 15. C.A. (Qld.), s. 2. C.A. (W.A.), s. 2.

[46]C.A. (S.A.), s. 5. Australian Constitutions Act (1850), s. 14. C.A. (Tas.), s. 10.

terms of the Australian States Constitution Act, 1907. They are:

(1) bills which alter the constitution of the legislature of the State or either House thereof,[47]
(2) bills which affect the salary of a Governor of a State,
(3) bills which are required to be reserved by an Act of the legislature of the State passed after 1907.[48]

It is further provided that the Act is not to affect those bills which are required to be reserved by Royal Instructions.[49] However, the Governor himself may assent to bills falling within these classes where his assent is given to a bill of a temporary nature because of "some public and pressing emergency" or where the Governor has previously received approval from the monarch to assent.[50]

Powers conferred by the Constitutions of the States on the Governor are as follows. He may summon and prorogue[51] the Houses of Parliament and dissolve the Lower House[52] and, in certain States, the Upper House when a deadlock occurs.[53] He appoints the ministers of the Crown.[54] No money is to be appropriated by Act or resolution unless first recommended by the Governor to the Lower House[55] and no part of the revenue is to be issued except by warrant of the Governor.[56] Standing orders passed by both Houses of Parliament are to be approved by him before coming into force.[57] In four of the States

[47] But not a bill which alters the composition of, or electoral provisions pertaining to, such Houses, s. 1 (2).
[48] Apart from the Constitution Acts, the requirement of reservation in State enactments is rare. A reserved bill does not come into force until the Governor signifies by message to the legislature or by proclamation that the bill has been assented to by the monarch: Australian Constitutions Act (1842), s. 33. It is submitted that the question of reservation is today merely a formality and that the monarch would, in assenting to the reserved bill, act on the advice of the ministers of the State in which the bill was passed (forwarded through the Commonwealth Office). It has been suggested, however, that a reserved bill might not be assented to where the Commonwealth Government tendered advice to that effect on the ground that the bill would be inimical to the interests of Australia as a whole. See A. C. Castles, "Limitations on the Autonomy of the Australian States", *Public Law* (1962), 195.
[49] See Clause VII of these Instructions (Appendix V).
[50] S. 1 (1), provisos (b) and (c).
[51] I.e. adjourn parliament at the end of a session.
[52] C.A. (N.S.W.), s. 10. C.A. (Vic.), s. 8, s. 20. C.A. (S.A.), s. 6. C.A. (Tas.), s. 12. C.A. (Qld.), s. 12. C.A. (W.A.), s. 6.
[53] Victoria and South Australia.
[54] C.A. (N.S.W.), s. 47. C.A. (Vic.), s. 50(1). C.A. (S.A.), s. 68. C.A. (Qld.), s. 14. C.A. (W.A.), s. 74.
[55] C.A. (N.S.W.), s. 46. C.A. (Vic.), s. 63. C.A. (S.A.), s. 59. C.A. (Tas.), s. 38. C.A. (Qld.), s. 18. C.A. Amendment Act (W.A.), s. 46 (8).
[56] C.A. (N.S.W.), s. 44. C.A. (Vic.), s. 93. C.A. (S.A.), s. 71. C.A. (Qld.), s. 19. C.A. (W.A.), s. 68.
[57] C.A. (N.S.W.), s. 15 (2). C.A. (S.A.), s. 55 (2). C.A. (Tas.), s. 17 (2). C.A. (Qld.), s. 8. C.A. (W.A.), s. 43.

judges are removable by the Queen on an address by the legislature; in the other two States by the Governor on an address by the legislature.[58] In some States the Governor is given the power to recommend to Parliament that amendments be made to bills presented to him for assent.[59] Under the Letters Patent constituting the office of Governor, further powers are granted including the power of making grants of Crown land, appointing judges, granting pardons, and suspending or removing officials holding office by royal Commission or warrant. Besides the powers which are conferred on the Governor by these constitutional instruments, the Governor in Council is given numerous powers under State laws.

In most cases the powers conferred must, in accordance with the doctrine implicit in the Constitution Acts and derived from convention, be exercised by the Governor on the advice of the ministers of the Crown of the particular State.[60] It would be contrary to constitutional convention for the Governor to act contrary to the advice of those ministers.[61] It is true that, at least in those States where ministerial office does not automatically entail membership of the Executive Council, the Governor could appoint to the Council individuals who did not have the support of the majority of members of Parliament. But, as Jenks points out, such a Council would be useless. "It could expend no money, carry out no policy and it would, in effect, be a mere nullity."[62] In other words the government of the State would collapse. Conse-

[58]Removal by the Sovereign: N.S.W. Supreme Court Act 1900, s. 10. C.A. (S.A.), s. 75. C.A. (Qld.), s. 16. C.A. (W.A.), s. 55. Removal by the Governor: C.A. (Vic.), s. 77. Tasmanian Supreme Court (Judges Independence) Act, s. 1. See Z. Cowen and D. P. Derham, "The Independence of Judges", 26 *Australian Law Journal* (1952-53), 462. The authors discuss the question whether an Imperial act passed in the eighteenth century entitled the *Colonial Leave of Absence Act* (popularly known as Burke's Act) still applies to the States. This Act provides an alternative procedure for removing a judge: "amotion" by the Executive Council of the State, with the judge having a right of appeal to the Privy Council.

[59]C.A. (Vic.), s. 14. C.A. (S.A.), s. 56.

[60]It is expressly provided in s. 71 of the South Australian Constitution Act that an order of the Governor involving expenditure of money or appointment to or dismissal from office is not valid unless it is countersigned by the Chief Secretary.

[61]Of course, so far as the power of appointing ministers is concerned, if a ministry is defeated at an election, the power of appointing the new ministry would not be dependent on the advice of the outgoing Premier but on the advice of the leader of the group which obtained the support of a majority of members in the new Parliament and who is consequently commissioned to form a Government. The leader of the ministry of a State (who is called the Premier) has by constitutional convention the right to nominate his ministers. For a discussion of the pre-eminent place of the Premier as evidenced by an earlier precedent see R. P. Roulston, "Dismissal of Ministers of the Crown—a Tasmanian Precedent", 1 *Tasmanian University Law Review* (1959), 280.

[62]*The Government of Victoria*, p.271.

quently the Governor must act through those ministers who have the support of Parliament and who can marshal support in the Houses for the legislative programme which will enable them to govern. It is true that he has the right "to be consulted, to encourage and to warn" but the decision does not rest with him. In effect, most decisions as to the exercise of the powers conferred on the Governor by the Constitution Act or otherwise are made by that body or group of individuals who hold office with the support of Parliament and who, for that reason, are formally invested with ministerial office by the Governor and summoned to the Executive Council. That body, which is known as the Cabinet, meets regularly and reaches decisions not only on day-to-day matters of administration but also on the more fundamental matters which are formally entrusted to the Governor by the Constitution Acts: for example, the summoning of Parliament, recommendations as to the appropriation of revenue, etc. The Executive Council exists mainly to put into official form decisions which have been arrived at elsewhere. In that body, "the decisions of the Cabinet are put into official form, appointments confirmed, resignations accepted and proceedings ordered, and notices published."[63] This outward form must be followed to satisfy the requirements of formal law: the decision of the Cabinet will be affirmed by the Executive Council according to constitutional convention which as one writer has put it, "inhabits the twilight between mere practice and formal law".[64]

Higinbotham, C.J., had been very disturbed by the form of the Royal Instructions which empowered the Governor to act contrary to the advice of his ministers. In his view the Royal Instructions which empowered the Governor to act in this way were invalid as being contrary to the Victorian Constitution Act.[65] But it is quite clear that the Constitution Acts of the States, as we have pointed out, are incomplete

---

[63] *Ibid.*, p.275. The most formal process is the Order in Council.

[64] Anderson, "The Constitutional Framework", p.11. There are, however, some important differences between decisions of Cabinet and acts of the Executive Council. See G. Sawer, "Councils, Ministers and Cabinets in Australia", *Public Law* (1956), 110, and Enid Campbell, "Admissibility of Proceedings in Cabinet", 1 *Tasmanian University Law Review* (1959), 270. See also *Tonkin* v. *Brand* [1962] W.A.R. 1. For a general study in the operation of cabinet government in Australia, see Encel, *Cabinet Government in Australia*.

[65] Whatever the position in the nineteenth century was, it is quite true today that these Instructions, which were re-drafted in 1900 and again in 1925, are archaic in form and if literally interpreted would place in the Governor's hands far more power that he would exericse today. They must be regarded as modified by the conventional rule of ministerial responsibility, admitting of course the possibility of the exercise of certain reserve powers. See M. C. Harris and J. R. Crawford, "The Powers and Authorities Vested in Him", 3 *Adelaide Law Review* (1969), 303 at pp.312 *et seq.*

and do not specify the content of the executive power of the States and the circumstances in which it may be exercised. Quite apart from the numerous statutory enactments which confer powers on individual ministers or on the Governor in Council, the Acts merely set out the most important powers which are at the basis of the constitutional structure such as those pertaining to the dissolution of Parliament, appointment of ministers, appropriation of revenue. Over and above these powers, there are those which exist by implication as necessary to promote the peace, order, and good government of the State.[66] The two cases decided on the nature of implied State executive power—*Toy* v. *Musgrove*[67] and *Colonial Treasurer of New South Wales* v. *Joseph*[68]—although they deny the existence of the State executive powers in the circumstances, can be explained on the ground that in both cases the executive powers claimed were reserved to a different Executive. In *Toy* v. *Musgrove* the executive power of excluding aliens was regarded by the majority as at that time still part of the Imperial prerogative,[69] while in *Colonial Treasurer of New South Wales* v. *Joseph* it was held that the war prerogative was exclusively vested in the Commonwealth Executive.

Of course, such executive powers are always subject to statutory abridgment and control as well as to parliamentary supervision; they do not in any case extend to measures such as the imposition of taxation or interference with the liberty of the subject which must be sanctioned by Parliament.[70]

If we accept the fact that the Constitution Acts do not in themselves describe the circumstances under which the executive power may be exercised, we must look for the answer to the question in constitutional convention. It is accepted by most authorities that the Governor is not obliged to act on the advice of his ministers in all cases whatsoever. He possesses certain reserve powers which he must exercise constitutionally and not arbitrarily.[71] It is however very uncertain to

---

[66] On the vesting of the proprietary prerogatives of the Crown in the colonial executives, see the judgment of Stephen, J. in *New South Wales* v. *Commonwealth* (1976) 8 A.L.R. 1 at 67, but as to rights in the territorial sea see below, pp. 86-87.

[67] (1888) 14 V.L.R. 349.

[68] (1916) 25 C.L.R. 32.

[69] Cf. *Robtelmes* v. *Brenan* (1906) 4 C.L.R. 395. *Attorney-General for Canada* v. *Cain and Gilhula* (1905-6) 22 T.L.R. 757.

[70] In *Johns and Waygood Ltd.* v. *Utah Australia Ltd.* [1963] V.R. 70, it was recognized that the Executive had a prerogative power to establish commissions of enquiry subject to the qualification that the operation of such a commission would not interfere with the administration of justice in the ordinary courts.

[71] See Evatt, *The King and His Dominion Governors*, chap. 1.

which powers this individual prerogative of the Governor applies. There is at least strong authority for the proposition that in the exercise of the power to dissolve Parliament the Governor may in certain circumstances refuse to act on the advice of his ministers.[72]

At the outset, we must face a question of great difficulty—is the position of the Governor of the State to be equated with that of the Governor-General of the Commonwealth and in turn is the position of the Governor-General to be equated with that of the Queen in respect of the exercise of prerogative powers in the United Kingdom? If these equations are made, the exercise of the reserve power today has an exceedingly small compass.[73] In a work on the British Constitution[74] the view is expressed that the positions of the Queen and the Governor-General are dissimilar:

> The essential point to remember is that a Governor-General is nowadays appointed for a limited term on the advice of the Commonwealth government concerned, and thereafter acts on the advice of the Commonwealth ministers, and not on the advice or instruction either of the ministers or monarch in the United Kingdom. It follows that his involvement in controversy concerns himself alone, and not necessarily the place of the Crown. The temporary and appointive nature of his office, moreover, means that the real or apparent partisanship of any one incumbent need imperil nothing more than his own tenure. Neither of these statements can be safely made about the monarch personally.[75]

On the other hand there is the express statement issuing from the Imperial Conference of 1926 that the Governor-General of a Dominion is the representative of the Crown, holding in all essential respects the same functions in relation to the administration of public affairs in the Dominion as the monarch holds in Great Britain.[76] Commenting on this declaration, Evatt expresses the opinion that although significant in relation to dominion status it does not contain "any final solution of the various problems of the reserve power although it is recognized that the general principle of ministerial responsibility governs the actions of the King and Governors alike".[77]

[72] See the list of authorities cited *ibid.*, chap. 28.
[73] See Jennings, *Cabinet Government,* chap. 13, especially pp.427-28.
[74] G. Marshall and G. C. Moodie, *Some Problems of the Constitution* (4th rev. ed.; London: Hutchinson, 1967). p.46.
[75] *Ibid.,* p.53.
[76] Cmd. 2768, par. IV (b), p.560.
[77] *The King and his Dominion Governors,* p.193. See also, "The Discretionary Authority of Dominion Governors", 18 *Canadian Bar Review* (1940), 1, 1-2.

The office of State Governor is not in all respects similar to the office of Governor-General. The Governor is appointed by the Queen on the advice of the Foreign and Commonwealth Office[78] while the Governor-General is appointed by the Queen on the advice of the Federal Government.[79] Communications between a State and the Queen usually go through the Foreign and Commonwealth Office, while the normal channel of communication between the Commonwealth and Queen is through a High Commissioner.[80] Furthermore, it must be pointed out that the Imperial conferences leading up to the enactment of the Statute of Westminster and to the conferment of legal independence on the Commonwealth did not include representatives of the States and in fact the Statute did not confer legal independence on the States.[81] As a matter of formal law therefore the position of the State Governor differs from that of the Governor-General.[82] Evatt, however, does not consider these differences significant. It is his view that within their respective spheres of authority the State Governors are just as much the representatives of the monarch for State purposes as the Governor-General is for Commonwealth purposes. And, as far as the Statute of Westminster is concerned, it was not concerned with the task of expressing "the relative constitutional position either of the State Governor and State Ministers, or of the Commonwealth Governor-General and Commonwealth Ministers".[83]

Precedents in recent years relating to the exercise of the power to refuse a request for dissolution suggest that State Governors possess a degree of discretionary authority in this area.[84] Indeed, in relation to a particular request for the dissolution of the Tasmanian House of Assembly the Governor, while granting the dissolution, expressly rejected the view that the exercise of his discretion should be confined to "ex-

[78] The wishes of the State Government on the appointment would be met. See p.70, n. 38.

[79] Anderson, "The Constitutional Framework", pp.13-14.

[80] *Ibid.*, p.14.

[81] The Colonial Laws Validity Act of 1865, one effect of which was to confirm that the Imperial Parliament held legal supremacy over the colonies, was only repealed so far as it affected legislation of the Commonwealth Parliament: s. 2, Statute of Westminster.

[82] See A. B. Keith, *The Dominions as Sovereign States* (London: Macmillan & Co., 1938), pp.208-9.

[83] *The King and his Dominion Governors*, pp.208, 212.

[84] See Enid Campbell, "The Prerogative Power of Dissolution: Some Recent Tasmanian Precedents", *Public Law* (1961), 16⁴. See also Encel, *Cabinet Government in Australia*, pp.74 *et seq.*

treme circumstances".[85]

However, it seems that (apart from extreme circumstances) this type of discretion will exist only in relation to a power to refuse a request for dissolution. In this type of case, the Governor is faced with a decision which requires weighing the right of Parliament to a continuance of its existence for the period specified in the Constitution Acts (assuming a new ministry can be found to replace that whose advice is rejected) against the right of a ministry to seek a verdict from the people when a change has occurred in the parliamentary situation or a major issue of public importance has arisen.[86] Automatic reliance on ministerial advice would lead to subversion of the principle that Parliament is prima facie entitled to continue in existence for the period laid down in the Constitution Acts.[87] Of course, if a Premier having the confidence of the Lower House advises the Governor to dissolve the House before the expiry of this period, the Governor, subject only to being satisfied that Supply is available, has no alternative but to act on such advice. Likewise where a ministry is defeated in the House and no alternative government is possible, the Governor can only act on the advice of the defeated Premier.

On the other hand, it is clear that, in the absence of express words[88] or a necessary implication that the Governor is not bound to exercise on ministerial advice the other powers conferred on him by the State Constitutions Acts or derived from other sources, he must act on such ministerial advice except in extreme circumstances. In these latter circumstances the Governor may resort to the ultimate remedy of dismissing the ministry or dissolving Parliament.[89] The extreme circum-

---

[85] See Comment, "The Australian States and Dominion Status", 31 *Australian Law Journal* (1957-58), 42; W.A. Townsley, "The Government of Tasmania", in Davis, ed., *The Government of the Australian States*, p.537; W.H. Craig, "The Governor's Reserve Power in Relation to the Dissolution of the Tasmanian House of Assembly", 1 *Tasmanian University Law Review* (1960), 488. In Victoria in 1952 requests for dissolutions from successive Premiers were refused although after the refusal to the second Premier the former Premier was recalled and granted a dissolution. The justification for the first refusal was that Supply had not been granted. (The Supply Bill had been defeated in the Upper House.) This would suggest that in all cases before a dissolution is granted a Governor will have to be satisfied that Supply has been granted. For the circumstances surrounding the refusals, see Encel, *Cabinet Government in Australia*, p.85; Fajgenbaum and Hanks, *Australian Constitutional Law* (1972), pp.84-85.

[86] See generally Harris and Crawford, "The Powers and Authorities Vested in Him", pp.321 *et seq.*

[87] I.e. three years in the case of the majority of the States.

[88] As in s. 41 (1) of the C.A. (S.A.).

[89] For an expression of the older view see A. Todd, *Parliamentary Government in the British Colonies* (London: Longmans, Green, 1880), p.40: "In the ordinary exer-

stances which would justify the exercise of such powers cannot be ex-haustively enumerated. However, Forsey's view of these circum-stances would seem to be too wide.[90] The principles which would justify the exercise of these powers may be summed up in the vague but meaningful phrase, "the rule of law". If a government were pursu-ing a policy based on a disregard for the fundamental principles on which our constitutional structure is founded (for instance, parliamen-tary supremacy or ministerial responsibility) and was, for example, at-tempting to rule without the support of Parliament[91] or contrary to its laws then that would justify a refusal to act on the advice of the government and also its dismissal.[92] And if a government, supported by a parliamentary majority, introduced legislation with the intention of destroying the system of parliamentary democracy, such as legisla-tion abolishing the party system or establishing a single party control-led by the government itself, such action would justify a refusal of as-

cise of his constitutional discretion, a Governor is unquestionably competent to reject the advice of his Ministers, whenever that advice should seem to him to be adverse to the public welfare, or of an injurious tendency." The requirement that the Governor must act on advice except in extreme circumstances would also be applicable to the Queen in respect of the exercise of her prerogative to give assent to reserved bills.

[90]E. A. Forsey, *The Royal Power of Dissolution of Parliament in the British Com-monwealth* (Toronto: Oxford University Press, 1943), p.470: " ... If the Crown were asked to 'swamp' the Upper House (in jurisdictions where such a power exists), or to assent to some major change in the electoral system, a widening or narrowing of the franchise, abolition of the ballot, abolition of the Upper House, or of the Monarchy, prolongation of the life of Parliament otherwise than by general consent, a change from private to social ownership of the means of production (or vice versa), then it might well insist that any such change should first be submitted to the judgement of the electors."

[91]In the federal sphere a dismissal of a Prime Minister occurred in November 1975 with the withdrawal by the Governor-General (Sir John Kerr) of the Commission of the Prime Minister (Mr. Whitlam) in circumstances where Supply had not been granted because of the non-passage of the Appropriation Bills by the Upper House and the refusal of the Prime Minister to resign or advise a general election. The Governor-General in giving his reasons for the dismissal indicated that, in a bicameral system with an Upper House constituted as a States' House which had the right to reject supply, the non-granting of supply had lead to a situation where his only course of action was to commission a caretaker Prime Minister who would obtain Supply and advise a dissolution.

[92]In 1932 the Governor of New South Wales, Sir Philip Game, dismissed the Lang ministry which persisted in acting contrary to the financial agreement and Common-wealth legislation giving effect to the agreement, entered into between the Com-monwealth and States, the sanction for which was to be found in the Commonwealth Constitution. Evatt criticizes the action of the Governor on the ground that the remedies available at law by action in the courts should have been exhausted before this drastic action was taken. See Evatt, *The King and his Dominion Governors*, chap. 19, especially pp.173-74. As against this it could be said that the previous con-duct of Mr. Lang had shown that he was prepared to disregard any ruling which would interfere with his policy and that, at a stage when civil violence was a distinct possibility, the Governor had acted properly in the circumstances.

sent to the legislation in question and a dissolution of Parliament. But this situation would really be a revolutionary one.

In summary, it is submitted that apart from the power to refuse ministerial advice to dissolve—a power which must necessarily inhere in the Governor as arbiter of the legal bonds which exist between the Executive and the legislature—all other powers which are conferred on the Governor without specifically vesting in him a discretion as to their execution must be exercised by the Governor on the advice of his ministry. Where, however, a government is set on a policy of subverting the constitutional structure, the extreme remedy of dismissal is available.[93] Likewise where a parliamentary majority is pursuing such a course the extreme remedy of a forced dissolution would be proper.[94] No doubt this solution leaves the nature of the reserve powers in an undefined state and withdraws from the courts (which of course can only enforce the law derived from formal sources) jurisdiction over the matter. Some writers, such as Evatt, have argued in favour of a formal statutory statement or restatement of the conventional practice governing the relationship between Crown, ministers, and Parliament, which would make this relationship justiciable.[95] The question whether the cause of constitutionality can better be served by a statutory definition of the powers of the Crown which would tend to certainty and inflexibility, or by convention which tends to flexibility but uncertainty, is one to which no final answer can be given at the present time.[96]

[93] The forced dismissal of a Ministry (i.e. a Premier and his Cabinet) must be distinguished from the dismissal of a particular Minister on the advice of a Premier supported by his Cabinet. See Roulston, "Dismissal of Ministers of the Crown—a Tasmanian Precedent", p.280. In such a situation convention would require that the Minister voluntarily tender his resignation.

[94] This would be justifiable on the basis that the rule of law is itself part of the constitutional law of the State and its ultimate sanction.

[95] The King and his Dominion Governors, p.289. The suggestion is that the legislature of a State could pass an enactment itself declaring the rules which are to regulate the powers of the Governor in respect of the appointment and dismissal of ministers and the dissolution of Parliament. But the validity of such an enactment would be in doubt as, in view of the fact that the Colonial Laws Validity Act still applies to the States, it might be said that this was an interference with the rights of the Crown recognized in Imperial legislation and therefore outside the legislative competence of the States. Enabling legislation of the Imperial Parliament might be necessary.

[96] The dismissal of the Prime Minister (Mr. Whitlam) by the Governor-General (Sir John Kerr) in 1975 (referred to on p.79 n.91) has led to intense discussion on the nature of the vice-regal reserve powers. Shortly after the dismissal, the South Australian Parliament resolved that a Governor should not exercise a reserve power of dismissal subject only to exceptions (a) where the Ministry had lost the confidence of the Lower House and refused to resign or recommend a dissolution, or (b) where an illegal act had been committed. This resolution cannot of course bind a future Governor in the exercise of his prerogative powers. No other State has passed a similar resolution.

CHAPTER FIVE

The Law-Making Power of the States

THE CONSTITUTION ACTS OF THE STATES grant to their legislatures general legislative power. In the case of New South Wales and Western Australia the grant is to make laws "for the peace, order and good government of the colony";[1] in the case of Victoria to make laws "in and for Victoria in all cases whatsoever";[2] and in the case of Queensland to make laws, "within Queensland, for the peace, welfare and good government of the colony".[3] In South Australia s. 5 of the Constitution Act does not confer direct legislative power but vests in Parliament the powers previously exercised by the old Legislative Council under the Australian Constitutions Act. The power conferred on the old Council by s. 14 of that Act is one to make laws for the "peace, welfare and good government of the colony". The Tasmanian Constitution Act in no section confers legislative power on Parliament. One must therefore have recourse to s. 14 of the Australian Constitutions Act to discover the nature of legislative power conferred on that body.[4] Legislative power is therefore conferred on the Tasmanian Parliament directly by Imperial enactment (the 1850 Act) and also in the case of Western Australia by Imperial enactment (the Act of 1889 as amended still being in force) but in the case of New South Wales, South Australia, Queensland, and Victoria by local enactment (the Acts of 1902, 1934, 1867, and 1975 respectively).[5]

The different wording in the provisions of these Acts conferring law-making power has no legal significance. In all cases a general power of law making is conferred subject to limitations arising from the Colonial Laws Validity Act and the territorial principle. In a number of cases decided in the nineteenth century the Privy Council adopted the view that acting within their constitutional powers the legislatures of the colonies had plenary authority: they were not delegates of the Imperial Parliament. Therefore, the principle *delegatus non potest*

---

[1] C.A. (N.S.W.), s. 5. C.A. (W.A.), s. 2.
[2] C.A., s. 16.
[3] C.A., s. 2.
[4] I.e. power to make laws for the peace, welfare, and good government of the State.
[5] See p.47.

delegare did not apply and they could delegate part of their authority to subordinate bodies.[6] However, a delegation which amounts to an abdication of power is invalid.[7]

EXTRATERRITORIAL LEGISLATIVE POWER

The conferment of power in the terms described above (peace, order or welfare, and good government) did not restrict the legislatures in deciding what laws would best fulfil their purposes. As Keith points out, "the means to the end are entirely for the judgement of the legislature which enacts; the test is subjective, not objective, and no Court can substitute its views of what should be enacted for those of the legislature".[8] However, the conferment of legislative powers in these terms has been regarded as at least having this limiting role: the legislation must be in some way associated with persons, things, or events being within or happening within the territory of the States. For many years after the advent of responsible government it was recognized that the legislatures could not enact legislation which had an extraterritorial effect. In an important Privy Council decision in the nineteenth century it was held that a bigamy provision of a New South Wales statute did not extend to marriages contracted by residents of the colony while abroad.[9] Although it has been argued that this decision was not intended to establish a doctrine of extraterritorial legislative incompetence and can be explained on grounds of statutory interpretation,[10] it has been recognized in a number of cases decided in the present century that the State Parliaments are subject to definite limitations in respect of their power of enacting legislation which has

---

[6] *R.* v. *Burah* (1878) 3 App. Cas. 889. *Hodge* v. *The Queen* (1884) 9 App. Cas. 117. *Powell* v. *Apollo Candle Co.* (1884) 10 App. Cas. 282. See also *Cobb & Co. Ltd.* v. *Kropp* (1966) 40 A.L.J.R. 177.

[7] *In re Initiative and Referendum Act* [1919] A.C. 935 at 945. *Commonwealth Aluminium Corporaton Ltd.* v. *Attorney-General for the State of Queensland* (Supreme Court of Queensland, not yet reported, Judgment of Wanstall, S.P.J.).

[8] A. B. Keith, *Responsible Government in the Dominions* (2nd ed.; Oxford: Clarendon Press, 1928), I, 320. See also *Riel* v. *The Queen* (1885) L.R. 10 A.C. 675.

[9] *Macleod* v. *Attorney-General for New South Wales* [1891] A.C. 455. On the question generally see D. P. O'Connell, "The Doctrine of Colonial Extraterritorial Legislative Incompetence", 75 *Law Quarterly Review* (1959), 318; T. P. B. Fry, *The International and National Competence of Australian Parliaments to Legislate in Respect of Extraterritorial Crime* (University of Queensland Faculty of Law Paper, Vol. I, No. 2, 1947); W. A. Wynes, *Legislative, Executive and Judicial Powers in Australia* (4th ed.; Sydney: Law Book Co., 1970), pp.64-69; A. C. Castles, "Limitations on the Autonomy of the Australian States", *Public Law* (1962), 196-201.

[10] J. W. Salmond. "The Limitations on Colonial Legislative Power", 33 *Law Quarterly Review* (1917), 117.

an extraterritorial effect.[11] The degree of connection with the territory of a State which a statute must have in order to make it a law for the peace, welfare, and good government of the State has not been finally determined, but it seems that a taxing act will only have effect if the property or person to be taxed is within the State[12] or, in the case of shares in a company incorporated outside the State, if the earnings derived therefrom by an individual not domiciled in the State are substantially related to the operations of the company within the State.[13] The mere presence of one extraterritorial element in a statute does not lead to invalidity if other elements in the statute are related to the territory of the State.[14]

In *Croft* v. *Dunphy*[15] anti-smuggling legislation of the Dominion of Canada was impugned on the ground that it applied to acts occurring outside the territorial waters of the Dominion[16]. It was held by the Judicial Committee of the Privy Council that the Dominion Parliament had full power to legislate with regard to such acts. At the time of commencement of the proceedings in this case, the Statute of Westminster, which conferred full extraterritorial power on Dominion Parliaments, was not in operation and consequently the Judicial Committee must be taken to have decided the issue with the older Macleod doctrine in mind. It could see "no reason to restrict the permitted scope of such legislation [of the Dominion] by any other consideration than is applicable to the legislation of a fully Sovereign State".[17]

To what extent is the *Croft* v. *Dunphy* principle, which is regarded as providing a more liberal test of "connection" than the Macleod principle, applicable to the Australian States, which have not been

---

[11]See, for example, *Commissioner of Stamp Duties (N.S.W.)* v. *Millar* (1932) 48 C.L.R. 618. *Broken Hill South Ltd.* v. *Commissioner of Taxation (N.S.W.)* (1936-37) 56 C.L.R. 337.

[12]*Thompson* v. *Commissioner of Stamp Duties (N.S.W.)* (1968) 42 A.L.J.R. 135. (H.C.) [1969] A.C. 320 (P.C.). Contrast *Johnson* v. *Commissioner of Stamp Duties (N.S.W.)* [1956] A.C. 331; *Welker* v. *Hewett* (1969) 120 C.L.R. 503; *Kolsky* v. *Mayne Nickless Ltd.* [1970] N.S.W.R. 511.

[13]*Commissioner of Stamp Duties (N.S.W.)* v. *Millar* (1932) 48 C.L.R. 618.

[14]See *Croft* v. *Dunphy* [1933] A.C. 156. *Ashbury* v. *Ellis* [1893] A.C. 339. *D.* v. *Commissioner of Taxes* [1941] St. R. Qd. 1, 218. With respect to acts performed abroad a State legislature can, subject to the Commonwealth Constitution, penalize *entry* into the territory after the commission of an act abroad and by this technique of draftsmanship overcome the obstacle presented by *Macleod's Case*. Moreover, the Imperial Parliament can confer power of an extraterritorial nature. It has in fact done so with regard to coastal trade in the Merchant Shipping Act (1894).

[15][1933] A.C. 156.

[16]The legislation applied *inter alia* to any vessel registered in Canada which was "hovering" within twelve miles of the coast and which had dutiable goods on board.

[17][1933] A.C., at p.163.

granted full extraterritorial power by the Statute of Westminister[18] and which are component units—with limited powers—of a federation? In *Trustees, Executors and Agency Co. Ltd.* v. *Federal Commissioner of Taxation*[19] there are dicta of Evatt, J., which suggest that it does apply to the States.[20] In *Broken Hill South Ltd.* v. *Commissioner of Taxation (N.S.W.)*[21] Dixon, J., phrased the limitation on State power in this way:

> ... It is within the competence of the State legislature to make any fact, circumstance, occurrence or thing in or connected with the territory the occasion of the imposition upon any person concerned therein of a liability to taxation or any other liability ... It is also within the competence of the legislature to base the imposition of liability on no more than the relation of the thing to the territory. The relation may consist in presence within the territory, residence, domicile or carrying on business there, or even remoter connections. If a connection exists it is for the legislature to decide how far it should go in the exercise of its powers.[22]

Recent cases display a tendency of the courts to depart from the narrow Macleod formulation and to adopt the more liberal test. Thus in *O'Sullivan* v. *Dejneko*[23] the High Court upheld the conviction of a South Australian resident for failing to supply information to the New South Wales Commissioner of Transport relating to journeys made by a vehicle owned by the "out of State" resident on roads in New South Wales as required by the New South Wales Road Maintenance (Contribution) Act.[24] In *R.* v. *Bull*[25] the High Court held that the Northern Territory Supreme Court had jurisdiction to hear and determine proceedings for offences against federal legislation occurring within three miles of the Northern Territory coast. Several judges in that case approved the application of the *Croft* v. *Dunphy* principle to

---

[18] This full power was granted to the Parliament of the Commonwealth.
[19] (1933) 49 C.L.R. 220.
[20] *Ibid.*, at pp.240-41.
[21] (1936-37) 56 C.L.R. 337.
[22] *Ibid.*, at p.375.
[23] (1963-64) 110 C.L.R. 498.
[24] See also *Ex parte Iskra* [1963] N.S.W.R. 1593; *Searles* v. *Searles* [1965] V.R. 83. Contrast, however, the Queensland case of *John Burke Ltd.* v. *The Insurance Commissioner* [1963] Qd.R. 587, where it was held that a Queensland Workers' Compensation Act did not apply to the employment of seamen on vessels plying between ports of the Queensland mainland, the Torres Strait Islands, and the Gulf of Carpentaria, the only connection of which with Queensland was that the vessels were registered in the State or owned by companies whose chief places of business were in the State. See also *Welker* v. *Hewett* (1969) 120 C.L.R. 503.
[25] (1974) 48 A.L.J.R. 232.

State legislative power.[26] To similar effect is the decision of the Full Court of Queensland in *Barnes* v. *Cameron*[27] which upheld the application of State regulations to a jetty extruding beyond the low-water mark. In *Giles* v. *Tumminello*,[28] the Supreme Court of South Australia upheld the conviction of a South Australian resident who had stolen crayfish pots in an area which lay four and a half miles from the South Australian coastline, that is, outside territorial waters;[29] while in *Munro* v. *Lombardo*[30] the Supreme Court of Western Australia held that fisheries legislation of that State applied to the possession of prohibited categories of fish by Western Australian residents which had been taken adjacent to the Western Australian coastline but outside territorial waters.[31] In both cases, the relevant connection to which the legislation attached was residence within the State associated with acts occurring on the "fringe" beyond territorial waters. In *Munro* v. *Lombardo*, however, the issue was complicated by the fact that the taking of the prohibited categories of fish occurred in an area which was subject to the Commonwealth Fisheries Act.[32]

In 1967 joint (or what has been described as "mirroring") legislation was enacted by the Commonwealth and the six States to control the exploration for and exploitation of petroleum resources in the maritime areas bounded by the low-water mark of the coastline (excluding, however, internal waters) and the outer edge of the continental shelf. It covers therefore both territorial waters (which at present extend to the three-mile limit)[33] and the continental shelf.[34] This legislation was

---

[26] Barwick, C. J. at p.243; Gibbs J. at p.256; Stephen J. at 240; Mason J. at p.264.
[27] [1975] Qd. R. 128.
[28] [1963] S.A.S.R. 96.
[29] In *R.* v. *Bull* (1974) 48 A.L.J.R. 232 at 244, Barwick, C. J. expressed the opinion that the case was wrongly decided. The basis for this opinion would appear to be that in the exercise of Admiralty jurisdiction outside territorial waters Imperial legislation applied. This also appears to be the view of Mason, J. (48 A.L.J.R. at p.264). On this matter see discussion of *R.* v. *Oteri* in text.
[30] [1964] W.A.R. 63.
[31] However, in *Green* v. *Burgess* [1960] V.R. 158 the Victorian Supreme Court held that a provision of the Victorian Fisheries Act was limited to the taking of fish within Victorian waters.
[32] This Act No. 7 of 1952 (as amended) applies to Australian waters *beyond* territorial limits. In *Bonser* v. *La Macchia* (1968-69) 122 C.L.R. 177, the High Court held that the Commonwealth Fisheries Act applied to waters adjacent to coastline but outside the three-mile limit.
[33] Many countries, however, claim a twelve-mile limit. The Convention on the Territorial Sea of 1958 contains clauses relating to the determination of baselines from which the territorial sea is measured (which would constitute the outer limit of internal waters). For a discussion of some of the issues involved see R. D. Lumb, *The Law of the Sea and Australian Off-Shore Areas* (St. Lucia: University of Queensland Press, 1966), chap. 3. The Convention also recognizes that coastal States may exercise

based on a co-operative arrangement under which the Commonwealth and States agreed that a common mining code would be applied to this area with a sharing of royalties from discoveries according to fixed proportions, with the States administering the code. The law in force in the adjacent State was applied to activities associated with exploration and exploitation of petroleum resources in the maritime area adjacent to that State.[35]

In 1973 the Commonwealth enacted the Seas and Submerged Lands Act (Act No. 161 of 1973) declaring and enacting that sovereignty in respect of the territorial sea (including airspace and seabed) was vested in the Crown in right of the Commonwealth.[36] The Act also vests in the Commonwealth sovereign rights over the continental shelf for the purpose of exploring and exploiting its natural resources. Section 16 of the Act provides that it does not (a) "limit or exclude the operation of any law of the Commonwealth or of a Territory in force at the date of commencement of this Act or coming into force after that date", and does not (b) "limit or exclude the operation

jurisdiction over a contiguous zone for certain purposes (e.g., pollution, customs). Such a zone may have a maximum extent of twelve miles. For an analysis of various questions arising in relation to maritime powers and jurisdiction see Sir Kenneth Bailey, "Law and the Oceans", *Australia's Neighbours*, Fourth Series, No. 71, 1970; R. D. Lumb, "The 1973 Law of the Sea Conference: Significant Issues", 7 *University of Queensland Law Journal* (1971) 256. International opinion now appears to be moving in favour of a 200 miles economic zone over which a nation will have "management" rights. This matter is being discussed at a new Law of the Sea Conference.

[34] The Article of the Convention on the Continental Shelf defines the shelf as referring "(a) to the seabed and subsoil of the submarine areas adjacent to the coast but outside the area of the territorial sea, to a depth of 200 metres, or beyond that limit to where the depth of the superjacent waters admits of the exploitation of the natural resources of the said areas; (b) to the seabed and subsoil of similar submarine areas adjacent to the coasts of islands".

[35] See Lumb, "The Off-Shore Petroleum Agreement and Legislation", 41 *Australian Law Journal* (1968) 453. "Sovereignty and Jurisdiction over Australian Coastal Waters", 43 A.L.J. (1969) 431.

[36] S. 1. To be read with s. 1 is s. 14 which provides: "Nothing in this Part affects sovereignty or sovereign rights in respect of any waters of the sea that are waters of or within any bay, gulf, estuary, river, creek, inlet, port or harbour and (a) were, on 1st January, 1901, within the limits of a State; and (b) remain within the limits of the State, or in respect of the airspace over, or in respect of the seabed or subsoil beneath, any such waters."

In *Bonser* v. *La Macchia* (1968-1969) 122 C.L.R. 177. two judges (Barwick, C.J. and Windeyer) relying on various cases including the English case of *R* v. *Keyn* (1876) 2 Ex.D. 63 considered that the Commonwealth had acquired sovereignty over territorial waters. Two other judges (Kitto and Menzies, J.J.) adhered to the view that the States had legislative power over territorial waters. See O'Connell, "The Australian Maritime Domain", 44 A.L.J. (1970) 192. The matter has now been determined in favour of the Commonwealth by the case of *New South Wales* v. *Commonwealth* (1976) 8 A.L.R. 1 (see discussion above).

of any law of a State in force at the date of commencement of this Act or coming into force after that date, except in so far as the law is expressed to vest or make exercisable any sovereignty or sovereign rights otherwise than as provided by the preceding provisions of this Part".

The Act was challenged by the six States in the High Court which, in a decision handed down in December 1975, upheld the validity of the Act: *New South Wales* v. *Commonwealth*.[37] All judges were agreed that the provisions relating to the continental shelf were valid. As to the territorial sea, the court split five-two, Barwick, C. J., McTiernan, Mason, Jacobs, and Murphy J.J. upholding the validity of the provisions relating thereto; Gibbs and Stephen J.J. dissenting. The majority held that the boundaries of the colonies ended at the low-water mark. Under the common law, moreover, *R*. v. *Keyn*[38] established that the territorial sea was not within the realm of England. Rights which a nation had, by virtue of international law, in the territorial sea were vested in the British Crown, not in the Crown in right of the colonies. Section 51 (xxix) of the Commonwealth Constitution vested in the Commonwealth Parliament power to make laws with respect to external affairs. Under this power the Commonwealth could legislate with respect to matters or things which were external to the continent of Australia. Likewise, it could give effect to international conventions (such as the Convention on the Territorial Sea) which related to such matters.

The judges forming the *minority* on this issue concluded that the States did have proprietary rights in the territorial sea before federation and that this area was part of the territory of the Crown. The Commonwealth could give effect to international conventions under the external affairs power but the particular provisions of the Act went beyond the Convention on the Territorial Sea in this respect, as the Convention was not concerned with the internal division of sovereignty between Commonwealth and States.

As a result of this decision, the Commonwealth has full power to legislate with respect to all matters and things affecting the territorial sea and sea bed (including fishing, mining, and crime). Until it does so, State laws will apply to adjacent maritime areas in so far as such laws are for the "peace, order, and good government of the State", and therefore a sufficient connection with the State is involved.[39]

[37](1976) 8 A.L.R. 1.
[38](1876) L.R. 2 Ex.D. 63.
[39]See *New South Wales* v. *Commonwealth* (1976) 8 A.L.R. 1 at 113-14 (Jacobs,

In respect of acts performed on or under the high seas (whether superjacent waters or subjacent seabed) adjacent to the coastline of a State but outside territorial waters, conflicts between Commonwealth and State jurisdiction, and also British Admiralty jurisdiction, are likely to occur. As to fishing there is no problem as Commonwealth legislation has been enacted in the Commonwealth Fisheries Act 1953-75 and the Continental Shelf (Living Natural Resources) Act 1968-73.

In respect of criminal acts occurring on the high seas there is considerable doubt whether State legislation applies and whether ordinary State jurisdiction operates. In *R.* v. *Oteri*[40] the Western Australian Supreme Court was concerned with an indictment alleging the commission of an offence (the theft of crayfish pots) committed on a "British ship" occurring 22 miles from the coastline "within the jurisdiction of the Admiralty of England". The Full Court held that Imperial legislation (the Admiralty Offences (Colonies) Act 1849 read with the Merchant Shipping Act 1894 and the Courts (Colonial Jurisdiction) Act 1874) was the source of the jurisdiction to try such an offence and that British law was applied. The result was that the British Theft Act of 1968 was applied.

This is clearly an unsatisfactory result and there appears to be a need to enact a Commonwealth law to cover all offences committed on the high seas outside territorial waters.[41]

It is clear that in the nineteenth century the purpose of the doctrine of colonial extraterritorial legislative incompetence was to safeguard the interests of the Imperial Parliament in matters of external and intercolonial affairs and to prevent violations of international law. It may be suggested that its basis today is the need to impose some restrictions on the legislative power of one State vis-a-vis another State in the Commonwealth, for otherwise there would be an overlapping of State legislative jurisdictions; while with respect to legislation having an effect outside Australian territory it may be suggested that under the Commonwealth Constitution the Federal Parliament is responsible for external affairs and therefore for acts and events which occur out-

---

J.). The High Court has recently upheld the application of Western Australian fisheries legislation in adjacent waters in *Pearce* v. *Florenca* (as yet unreported).

[40](1975) W.A.R. 120.

[41]*The Navigation Act* (Commonwealth) 1912-73, s. 381 applies to a portion of such offences. Some States, including Western Australia, have legislated to make applicable their criminal laws to acts of residents occurring in waters adjacent to the coastline or in circumstances where there are other connections with the State such as the use of State facilities, so as to overcome the *Oteri* decision.

side the territories of the States and which affect the relationship of Australia with other countries.[42]

Quite apart from this limitation on legislative power, it has always been recognized that the United Kingdom Parliament still retains ultimate legislative authority over the States. This authority is derived from s. 2 of the Colonial Laws Validity Act (1865). Before the enactment of the Colonial Laws Validity Act great uncertainty existed as to the authority of colonial Parliaments to enact legislation repugnant to British law. It was generally agreed that not only was the colonial legislature subject to British statute law applying to the colony but also to the fundamental rules of the common law. In South Australia this was the central issue in a constitutional crisis involving Mr. Justice Boothby of the Supreme Court and the South Australian legislature.[43] Mr. Justice Boothby had adopted a very wide test of repugnancy and was of the opinion that invalidity attached to portions of South Australian legislation which were contrary to what he regarded as principles of British constitutional law. Furthermore, Boothby, J., took the view that the failure to reserve bills which the Governor was obliged to reserve under Royal Instructions was a ground for invalidating those acts which had not been so reserved. The South Australian Government referred these judicial opinions to England for consideration and the law officers of the Crown advised that it was the duty of the Court to hold invalid legislation of the South Australian Parliament which was contrary to Imperial legislation extending to the colonies in general or to South Australia in particular, or contrary to fundamental principles of British law. On the other hand an act which

[42] This responsibility arises from a number of heads of power vested in the Commonwealth Parliament by s. 51 of the Commonwealth Constitution, e.g. powers over external affairs, interstate and overseas trade, industrial disputes extending beyond State limits. See R. v. *Foster ex parte Eastern and Australian Steamship Co. Ltd.* (1958-59) 103 C.L.R. 256. It may be suggested that a State cannot enact legislation contrary to the rules of international law for this would be a matter affecting Australia's relationship with other countries and therefore beyond its power. See G. V. La Forest, "May the Provinces Legislate in Violation of International Law", 39 *Canadian Bar Review* (1951), 78. In *Croft* v. *Dunphy* [1933] A.C., at p.165, the Privy Council adverted in passing to the possible limitations arising from international law.

[43] The circumstances which led to the request for advice by the South Australian Government and the report of the Imperial law officers (Collier and Palmer) on the basis of which the Colonial Laws Validity Act was drafted are to be found in E. S. Blackmore, *The South Australian Constitution* (Adelaide: Government Printer, 1894). p.64 *et seq.* A.J. Hannan, *The Life of Chief Justice Way* (Sydney: Angus & Robertson, 1960), chap. 4. Keith, *Responsible Government in the Dominions,* I, 339-49. See also D. B. Swinfen, "The Genesis of the Colonial Laws Validity Act", *Juridical Review* (1967), 29; Enid Campbell, "Colonial Legislation and the Laws of England", 2 *Tasmanian University Law Review* (1965) at pp.173-75.

altered non-fundamental principles should not be held invalid. Moreover, non-observance of Royal Instructions as distinct from an Act of Parliament requiring the reservation of bills was not a ground of invalidity as the Instructions were intended to be directory and not mandatory.[44] The South Australian Electoral Act of 1856, under which the two Houses of the South Australian Parliament had been constituted, had not been reserved as required by Imperial enactment and therefore subsequent legislation passed by the legislature, the members of which were elected on the basis of that Act, was invalid. To meet this problem, the Imperial Parliament passed validating acts, but when further doubt as to the legislative competence of the South Australian legislature arose, particularly in the area of constitutional amendment, the Imperial authorities decided to pass a general act clarifying the nature and extent of legislative power in the colonies. This act was the Colonial Laws Validity Act,[45] the most important effects of which were as follows. First of all the act defined the meaning of repugnancy. Colonial laws which were repugnant to an act of the Imperial Parliament extending to the colony by express enactment or by necessary intendment were void to the extent of repugnancy.[46] No colonial law was to be void on the ground that it was repugnant to the fundamental principles of English law.[47] On the question of the failure to reserve bills, the Act provided that bills were not to be void or inoperative because they had not been reserved in accordance with Instructions given to the Governor (other than Instructions contained in letters patent or other instrument authorizing the Governor to assent to bills).[48] Furthermore, it was declared that every colonial legislature should have the power to pass laws with respect to the constitution, powers or procedure of the legislature subject to the condition that such laws were to be passed in accordance with the manner and form laid down by existing law.[49] The Colonial Laws Validity Act, while enlarging the sphere of legislative authority of the colonies, in effect imposed two major restrictions on the powers of colonial Parliaments which survive today: (1) State legislation must not be repugnant to Imperial legislation extending to the States; (2) the States can only amend their constitutional laws of the nature specified in accordance

---

[44] Keith, *Responsible Government in the Dominions*, pp.339-40.
[45] 28 & 29 Vict., c.63.
[46] S. 2.
[47] S. 3.
[48] S. 4.
[49] S. 5.

with any manner and form that has been laid down in pre-existing law.

REPUGNANCY TO BRITISH LEGISLATION

A State act which conflicts with an act of the United Kingdom Parliament which has paramount force, that is to say, which applies to the State either by express words or by necessary intendment is, to the extent of the repugnancy, inoperative.[50] However, those limitations imposed by the original Constitution Acts on substantive power have been repealed or are no longer in force.[51] Moreover, it is clear that by convention the United Kingdom Parliament would not today pass any law affecting a State or States without the consent of the Parliament of that State.[52] There are, however, a number of enactments passed by the United Kingdom Parliament during the nineteenth century and the early part of this century which still bind the States. The first to be mentioned are of course the federating statute, the Commonwealth of

---

[50]It is probably not invalid for all time but may revive when the Imperial legislation with which it is inconsistent is repealed. For the application of the doctrine to Commonwealth legislation before the Statute of Westminister see *Union Steamship Co. of New Zealand Ltd.* v. *The Commonwealth* (1925) 36 C.L.R. 130. See also *Attorney-General for Queensland* v. *Attorney-General for the Commonwealth* (1915) 20 C.L.R. 148. In the latter case Higgins, J. said (p.178) that he was "strongly inclined to think that no Colonial Act can be repugnant to an Act of the Parliament of Great Britain unless it involves, either directly or indirectly or ultimately, a contradictory proposition—probably contradictory rights or contradictory duties". In the former case, however, Isaacs, J. (p.148) considered that "repugnancy" was equivalent to "inconsistency or contrariety". See A. C. Castles, "The Reception and Status of English Law in Australia", 2 *Adelaide Law Review* (1963), 29-31.

[51]They were superseded by subsequent Imperial legislation and the Commonwealth Constitution Act.

[52]Cf. *Copyright Owners Reproduction Society Ltd.* v. *E.M.I. (Australia) Ltd.* (1958) 100 C.L.R. 597, at p.612, per Dixon, C.J. This requirement is, of course, embodied in the Statute of Westminister in respect of Imperial legislation affecting the powers of the Commonwealth Parliament. S. 9 (2) of the Statute, however, which recognizes the possibility of Imperial legislation being enacted with regard to the States, does not expressly provide that the concurrence of the State(s) Parliament(s) is necessary. For a discussion of the possible operation of s. 9 see A. C. Castles, "Limitations on the Autonomy of the Australian States", pp.177-78. See also K. Bailey, "The Statute of Westminister", 5 *Australian Law Journal* (1932), 400. As to the meaning of the term "colony" as used in British Acts, see s. 11 of the Statute of Westminister (*infra*, p.126).

In *Rokov* v. *Bistricic* [1974] 2 N.S.W.L.R. 143 it was held that the *Merchant Shipping (Liability of Shipowners and Others) Act* of 1958 was not in force in New South Wales as it did not apply expressly or by necessary intendment to the Australian States. Indeed the practice of the United Kingdom Parliament as evidenced in s. 11 of that Act has been to exclude self-governing territories from the operation of the legislation. However, a State Act may provide for the adoption of later amendments by the United Kingdom Parliament to legislation in force in the State at federation. See *Australian Chamber of Shipping* v. *Maritime Services Board of New South Wales* [1974] 2 N.S.W.L.R. 197.

Australia Constitution Act,[53] and the Colonial Laws Validity Act.[54] Among other Imperial Statues in force are the Judicial Committee Acts, 1833 and 1844,[55] the Admiralty Offences (Colonies) Act, 1849,[56] the Courts (Colonial Jurisdiction) Act, 1874,[57] the Territorial Waters Jurisdiction Act, 1878,[58] the Colonial Courts of Admiralty Act, 1890,[59] the Merchant Shipping Act 1894,[60] and the Australian States Constitution Act, 1907.[61] The effect of s. 2 of the Colonial Laws Validity Act is to invalidate legislation of the States which is repugnant to the provisions of these Acts, and therefore, subject to the exception to be referred to, they cannot be repealed or amended by a State act.[62] It must be pointed out, however, that ordinary English legislation which was part of the heritage of English law introduced into Australia by virtue of s. 24 of the 1828 Act is subject to repeal in the same way as other State legislation under the powers conferred on the State legislatures to make laws for the peace, welfare, and good government of the States.[63]

[53] For a description of the effect of federation on the constitutional system of the colonies, see Lumb and Ryan, *The Constitution of the Commonwealth of Australia Annotated* (1974), pp. 1 *et seq.*, pp. 323 *et seq.* The main effects of the Commonwealth Constitution in the distribution of legislative power between Commonwealth and States were to make certain heads of power exclusive to the Commonwealth Parliament; with respect to another class of powers which is set out in s. 51 of the Constitution and which may be exercised concurrently by Commonwealth and States, it is provided by s. 109 that, in the event of inconsistency between a Commonwealth and a State law, the Commonwealth law prevails. The residue of legislative power which is not dealt with in either of these ways remains with the States (s. 107) (e.g. education, intrastate trade) but is subject to certain prohibitions imposed by the Constitution (e.g. s. 92). It is to be noted that a State act cannot bind the Commonwealth in the exercise of its prerogative rights: *Commonwealth of Australia* v. *Cignamatic Pty. Ltd.* (1962) 108 C.L.R. 372.

[54] Discussed in the present work.

[55] These Acts regulate appeals from State courts to the Privy Council (in matters of State jurisdiction).

[56] This Act confers jurisdiction on State courts for offences within Admiralty jurisdiction.

[57] This Act regulates the exercise of jurisdiction by State courts in the exercise of Admiralty criminal jurisdiction.

[58] This Act defines the jurisdiction of State courts in respect of offences occurring on foreign vessels in territorial waters.

[59] This Act establishes the jurisdiction of Australian courts in Admiralty and maritime matters.

[60] This enactment relates to the control of merchant shipping and navigation. Much of the ground is now covered by the Navigation Act 1912-73 (Commonwealth).

[61] Discussed in the present work.

[62] It seems, however, that under s. 51 (xxxviii) of the Commonwealth Constitution the Commonwealth Parliament may have power to legislate with respect to some of these matters with the concurrence of the Parliaments of all the States directly concerned. See G. Nettheim, "The Power to Abolish Appeals to the Privy Council from Australian Courts", 39 *Australian Law Journal* (1965), 39 at 44 *et seq.*

[63] When counsel argued that a Commonwealth Act was void as being inconsistent with Magna Carta, the High Court dismissed the argument by saying that it was not

In the case of some of the Imperial statutes referred to previously, powers of legislating (and in the case of the Merchant Shipping Act, of amendment of that Act) were given to the local legislatures subject to the requirement of reservation.

In *R. v. Commissioner for Transport ex parte Cobb & Co. Ltd.*[64] the Full Court of Queensland held that provisions of the Merchant Shipping Act, which conferred power over the "coasting" trade, empowered the legislature of Queensland to regulate the "coasting" trade of that State. Insofar as a Queensland transport act purporting to regulate the "coasting" trade within territorial waters did not contain a clause suspending its operation until royal assent had been publicly signified, the Act was struck down as being repugnant to s. 736 of the Merchant Shipping Act which imposed this requirement.[65] An appeal to the High Court of Australia went off on a different ground, although Dixon, C. J., said that the Queensland Parliament had ample authority to regulate the coasting trade within territorial waters under its general legislative power and therefore was not dependent on s. 736 of the Merchant Shipping Act for the exercise of this power.[66] It may be pointed out that the Judicial Committee of the Privy Council has given approval to the decision of the High Court.[67] It would seem, therefore, that s. 736 regulates coasting trade taking place *outside* territorial waters; and insofar as this is carried on between ports in one State only, the competent body with legislative authority under s. 736 would be the State Parliament concerned.[68]

APPEALS TO THE PRIVY COUNCIL: RELATIONS WITH THE UNITED KINGDOM

The period between 1973 and 1975 witnessed a continuing struggle between the Commonwealth Government and State Governments over the nature of the constitutional relations between Australian

---

worthy of serious consideration: *Chia Gee* v. *Martin* (1905) 3 C.L.R. 649. However, in *See* v. *Australian Agricultural Company* (1910) 10 S.R. (N.S.W.) 690 the New South Wales Full Court considered that a provision in a New South Wales Act was void insofar as it purported to repeal a requirement in a pre-1828 Imperial act which expressly extended to New South Wales. In 1969 the New South Wales Parliament passed an Imperial Acts Application Act (No. 30 of 1969). This Act specifies the pre-1828 legislation still in operation in New South Wales.

[64] [1963] Qd. R. 547.

[65] But see p.102.

[66] See *Kropp* v. *Cobb & Co. Ltd.* (1963) 36 A.L.J.R. 205.

[67] *Western Transport Pty. Ltd.* v. *Kropp* (1964) 38 A.L.J.R. 237.

[68] See judgment of Wanstall, J., in *Cobb's Case* [1963] Qd.R. 547, at pp.571 *et seq.*, especially pp.577-82.

Governments and the United Kingdom. It revolved around the question as to which government (Commonwealth or State) has the right to advise the Monarch (Her Majesty Queen Elizabeth the Second) in relation to all matters of an Australian Constitutional or governmental nature. A matter which also generated conflict was the question of appeals and special references in matters of State law to the Judicial Committee of the Privy Council.

The passage of the *Royal Style and Titles Act* by the Commonwealth Parliament in 1973 brought about a modification of the title Queen Elizabeth. In place of the older title embodied in the predecessor to that Act (the Act of 1952) which referred to the Queen as the Queen of the United Kingdom, Australia, and her other Realms and Territories, the new title omitted a reference to the United Kingdom. It was arguable therefore that the new designation of the Queen as Queen of Australia could support the thesis that in matters of Australian (whether Federal or State) constitutional law or convention, the sole advisers to Her Majesty would in future be Her Majesty's Australian Ministers (viz. the Ministers of the Commonwealth Government) and that the traditional connection between the States and the Monarch in matters of State constitutional power had been overridden.

In this period various States had taken steps to seek an advisory opinion from the Judicial Committee under s.4 of *Judicial Committee Act* of 1833 (Imperial) on the question of sovereignty and jurisdiction over adjacent coastal waters and the seabed. The Commonwealth Government objected to the requested reference and the United Kingdom Government decided that the matter should not be referred. It would appear that one reason for the rejection was that the *Seas and Submerged Lands Act* (No. 161 of 1973) has been passed by the Federal Parliament. There was therefore a justiciable matter involving the extent of Commonwealth and State powers which could be determined in the High Court of Australia. (Subsequently in 1974 the States challenged this legislation in the High Court.)

The central issue however in this confrontation concerned the States' traditional right of access to the Queen through the British Government. It appeared that the Commonwealth had taken the view that relations between Australia (considered as a whole or in terms of its component political units) fell within the province of the external affairs power (s. 51 (xxix) of the Commonwealth Constitution) and therefore were subject to paramount Commonwealth legislative and executive power. This argument involves the view that the stand taken by the British Government in the British-Australian negotiations relating to the Vondel incident[69] was applicable to relations between Her Majesty's British Government and Her Majesty's Australian Government concerning State constitutional or judicial matters and that this involved an exclusive, or at least paramount, competence on the part of the Commonwealth Government to give advice on such matters.

The objection to this viewpoint is that relations between the Executive Governments of the States and the Queen are part of the Constitutions of the States preserved by s. 106 of the Commonwealth Constitution.[70]

To counter the Commonwealth initiatives the States re-affirmed their right of access by the despatch of State government representatives to the United Kingdom to discuss and present State advice in current matters of concern. Some placed the position of Agent General on a statutory basis with the right to represent the State in overseas matters affecting its peace, welfare, and government (such as tourism, trade, immigration).[71]

In 1973 the Queensland Parliament enacted an *Appeals and Special Reference Act*.[72] Section 3(1) of this Act provided that the Queen could refer to the Judicial Committee of the Privy Council for hearing and consideration any question or matter to which the section related, "and the Judicial Committee may therefore hear and consider the same and advise Her Majesty thereon".[73] Section 3(2) provided that

the questions and matters to which this section relates are questions or matters which, whether as part of any cause or otherwise, and whether in the course of any proceedings in any Court in Queensland or otherwise, arise under or concern any law in force in Queensland (including the prerogatives of Her Majesty in right of Queensland) or which otherwise substantially relate to the peace, welfare and good government of Queensland.

[69] See Sawer, *Australian Federal Politics and Law,* 1901-1929, Vol. 1, pp.31-32. The incident involved the question whether a State Government should have provided assistance to a Consul of a foreign country under the terms of an international convention. Negotiations were conducted by the United Kingdom Government through the Governor-General. But the point at issue concerned the channel of communication on matters of external affairs, namely, the observance of treaties.

[70] Quick and Garran, *The Annotated Constitution of the Commonwealth of Australia,* pp.929-32.

[71] See for example, *Agent-General for Queensland Act* No. 2 of 1975.

[72] No. 42 of 1973.

[73] This provision incorporated substantially the subject matter of s. 4 of the *Judicial Committee Act* (Imp.) of 1833.

Section 4 empowered the Attorney-General, in relation to such matters, to apply to the Full Court of Queensland for an order granting a certificate that any question or matter was of the nature outlined and which by reason of its great general or public importance, or otherwise, ought to be referred to the Judicial Committee. The Court could grant the certificate (in terms specified by the Attorney-General or with amendments) or refuse the grant. If it refused the grant or granted the certificate on amended terms the Attorney-General could appeal to the Judicial Committee.

In 1974 the Attorney-General applied to the Full Court for a certificate that certain matters be referred to the Judicial Committee. They related to the capacity of the Queensland Parliament to adopt a Royal style and title for Queensland and the effect of the Commonwealth Royal Style and Titles Act of 1973 "on the manner in which or the extent to which Her Majesty is entitled to receive and act upon advice given to Her by Her Ministers of State in the United Kingdom and in Queensland in relation to matters affecting Queensland".

The Full Court granted the certificate and the State Governor then despatched to the Queen a request to refer the matters so certified to the Judicial Committee under the Act or under the Judicial Committee Act of 1833.

The validity of ss. 3 and 4 of the Queensland Act was challenged by the Commonwealth in the High Court. The High Court unanimously declared these provisions invalid.[74] The basis of the High Court's decision was that the provisions of the Act, which might enable reference of matters affecting the distribution of power between Commonwealth and States, or involving the interpretation of Commonwealth legislation, were inconsistent with the Judicature Chapter (chap. III) of the Commonwealth Constitution (particularly s. 74) which vested in the High Court ultimate authority to decide questions of a federal nature involving Commonwealth—State relations.

However, Gibbs J. in a judgment concurred in by three other members of the Court also considered arguments advanced by the Commonwealth that the legislation was invalid on extraterritorial grounds or as being repugnant to the Judicial Committee Act of 1833.[75] He rejected both arguments. Legislation of a State conferring

---

[74]*Commonwealth of Australia* v. *State of Queensland* (1975) 7 A.L.R. 351.
[75]Reliance was placed on *Nadan* v. *The King* [1926] A.C. 482.

jurisdiction on the Judicial Committee was not open to the objection that it failed to bear a sufficient relationship to the peace, welfare, and good government of the territory of the State. As far as the repugnancy argument was concurred, Gibbs, J. referred to the decision in *Woolworths (New Zealand) Ltd.* v. *Wynne*[76] where the New Zealand Court of Appeal held that it was competent to grant leave to appeal to the Judicial Committee under local legislation. State legisla tion enlarging the power or jurisdiction of the Judicial Committee was not to be regarded as repugnant to the Judicial Committee Act.

The Commonwealth Government in this period introduced legislation in the form of a *Privy Council (Abolition of Appeals) Bill* to abolish appeals from State Supreme Courts in State matters to the Judicial Committee but the legislation was on several occasions rejected by the Senate. The legislation, first introduced in 1973, contained two substantive provisions: one purporting to abolish appeals by force of Commonwealth legislative power (presumably s. 51 (xxix) of the Commonwealth Constitution—the external affairs power) and the other relying on the "request and consent" procedure contained in s. 4 of the Statute of Westminster by requesting and consenting to the enactment by the United Kingdom Parliament of legislation abolishing appeals from State courts.

Both provisions raised important questions namely (a) whether the external affairs powers covered relations between the States and United Kingdom Governments and in particular extended to the abolition of a right of appeal in State jurisdiction, and (b) in the light of sections 8 and 9 of the Statute of Westminster whether the request and consent procedure extended to a matter which was part of a State's Constitutional system.[77] However, it would appear that the dicta of Gibbs, J. referred to earlier suggest that appeals from State courts to the Privy Council in matters of State jurisdiction are within State authority and, therefore, are not an "external affair". With the defeat of the Bill in the Senate, the questions did not come up for judicial determination.

---

[76] [1952] N.Z.L.R. 496.
[77] See *McCawley* v. *R.* (1918) 26 C.L.R. 9 at 51-52 per Isaacs and Rich J. J. The judges adopted a meaning of the phrase "State Constitution" as comprising its judicial structure. However, Sawer, *The Australian Constitution* (Canberra: Australian Government Publishing Service, 1975) at p.119 considers that the external affairs power would be a basis for a request by the Commonwealth for the enactment of legislation by the United Kingdom Parliament.

MANNER AND FORM REQUIREMENTS: THE STRUCTURE OF THE LEGISLATURE

It will be convenient at the outset to set out in full the relevant part of s. 5 of the Colonial Laws Validity Act which imposes the "manner and form" limitation. It is as follows:

> Every representative legislature shall, in respect to the colony under its jurisdiction, have, and be deemed at all times to have had, full power to make laws respecting the constitution, powers and procedure of such legislature; provided that such laws shall have been passed in such manner and form as may from time to time be required by any act of parliament, letters patent, order in council, or colonial law for the time being in force in the said colony.

The effects of the section are to confirm that a colonial representative legislature[78] has full power to legislate with respect to a certain class of constitutional laws but to provide that those laws must be passed in the manner and form required by previous law (whether of Imperial or of local origin). At the time of the passage of the Act all the Australian legislatures except that of Western Australia had representative legislatures and therefore came within the immediate operation of the Act. Western Australia at a later date came within its operation when it received this form of government. Therefore, at the present time all the legislatures of the Australian States are invested with the power conferred, and subject to the restriction imposed, by s. 5.

It must be made clear that s. 5 of the Act is not the sole source of State legislative power. Ordinary legislative power and power in respect of constitutional matters were conferred by the original constitution acts which conferred responsible government on the Australian colonies. The purpose of s. 5 was to set aside doubts that had arisen as to the powers of the South Australian Parliament to amend laws relating to its constitution, powers and procedure, and to establish that all representative legislatures possessed such a power with respect to the class of laws affected by the section. In the cases of *Taylor* v. *Attorney-General for Queensland,*[79] *Trethowan* v. *Attorney-General for New South Wales,*[80] and *Clayton* v. *Heffron*[81] the courts emphasized that s. 5 applied only to laws respecting the constitution,

---

[78]Defined by s. 1 as a legislative body of which one-half are elected by inhabitants of the colony.
[79](1916-17) 23 C.L.R. 457.
[80](1930-31) 44 C.L.R. 394 (High Court); [1932] A.C. 526 (Privy Council).
[81](1960-61) 105 C.L.R. 214.

powers, and procedure of the legislature and this limitation was also recognized in the *South Eastern Drainage Board Case*,[82] where the requirement in a Real Property Act that future legislation should not be taken to have amended that Act, unless such an effect was expressly stipulated, was held not to have had any effect on a later Drainage Act which modified the operation of the Real Property Act without express mention. Unfortunately, the members of the High Court in this latter case, although reaching the right conclusion, did so by means of a process of reasoning which may be questioned. They posed the problem in the following manner: was the provision in the Real Property Act a law respecting the constitution, powers or procedure of the legislature?[83] In terms of strict logic, this question ought to have been asked of the later legislation—the Drainage Act—for s. 5 requires only the later legislation to be of this nature if it is to be subject to a manner and form requirement laid down in pre-existing law. Drainage legislation of course falls completely outside this category.[84]

In *Commonwealth Aluminium Corporation Limited* v. *Attorney-General for Queensland*[85] the Full Court of Queensland was concerned with a challenge to a Mining Royalties Act of 1974 (and regulations made thereunder) which purported to vary the rate of royalties payable on minerals extracted by the plaintiff company in areas leased by it from the Government. A prescribed method of determining the royalties was contained in an Agreement made between the state of Queensland and the Company to which legal force was given by the Commonwealth Aluminium Corporation Agreement Act of 1957. A section of that Act provided that the agreement could be varied pursuant to an agreement between the responsible Minister and the company which was approved by the Governor in Council and that "any purported alteration of the Agreement not made and approved in such manner shall be void and of no legal effect whatsoever." Any variation approved in this way which was not disallowed by the Legislative Assembly was to have the force of law as though it was an enactment of this Act. The plaintiff argued inter alia that the

---

[82] *South Eastern Drainage Board (South Australia)* v. *Savings Bank of South Australia* (1939-40) 62 C.L.R. 603.

[83] *Ibid.*, at pp.618, 623, 625, 636.

[84] It might be argued that the later amending or repealing Act is characterized as a law respecting the powers of the legislature in that it purports to affect the earlier legislation respecting its powers. See Fajgenbaum and Hanks, *Australian Constitutional Law* (Butterworths, 1972), p.286.

[85] 1974, as yet unreported.

variation purporting to have been made by the 1974 Act had not been passed in the prescribed manner and form.

A majority of the Court held that the Mineral Royalties Act was a valid act. It was considered that the relevant clause in the earlier Act was not a manner and form provision of the type given binding force by the *Colonial Laws Validity Act* as it was directed to the Executive Government and not to the Legislature. Wanstall, S. P. J. considered that if it were characterized as such a provision it would have infringed the basic doctrine that a Legislature cannot create and endow with its own capacity a new legislative power not created by the Act to which it owed its own existence.[86]

It is submitted that a State legislature has only a limited power under s. 5 of the Colonial Laws Validity Act to control its successor: limitations as to manner and form will apply only to future legislation respecting the constitution, powers or procedure of the legislature. Legislation of this type takes the form of provisions regulating the duration of the legislature, its nature, composition and membership, the relationship between the Houses of the legislature, the powers of the legislature to enact legislation, the procedure of the legislature (powers of the Speaker, size of a quorum, etc.), the privileges and immunities of the Houses, including the power to make standing orders, and requirements as to the passage of bills (majorities, reservation, referenda). S. 5 cannot be used to impose any manner and form requirement as to ordinary legislation or constitutional legislation falling outside this category. It may be pointed out that a Bill of Rights which gives protection to civil rights (such as life, liberty, and property) and which imposes a manner and form requirement (such as a referendum) for the passage of inconsistent legislation could not operate under s. 5 of the Colonial Laws Validity Act to affect or control later legislation inconsistent with the Bill of Rights, for the reason that the later legislation would have been characterized as legislation on specific matters[87] and not as legislation relating to the constitution, powers or procedure of the legislature.

The three cases cited previously in which s.5 of the Colonial Laws Validity Act was applied dealt with bills altering (or rather abolishing) the constitutions of State Upper Houses. In *Trethowan's Case* the re-

---

[86]See in *In re the Initiative and Referendum Act* [1919] A.C. 935, at 945.
[87]It is difficult, therefore, to see how the Commonwealth Powers Act, (Queensland) (1943), s. 3 could have controlled the manner and form of enacting legislation of the nature specified in that Act under s. 5 of the Colonial Laws Validity Act.

quirement as to manner and form under discussion was the submission of such a bill to a referendum while in *Taylor's Case* and *Clayton* v. *Heffron* the requirement pertained to a deadlock procedure (which included a referendum) designed to resolve conflicts between the Upper and Lower Houses. Such requirements were held to fall within the operation of s. 5 which therefore is wide enough to sanction not only procedural changes within the Houses of Parliament but also the modification of the component parts of the legislative body either by the introduction of an additional part (the electorate) or the abolition of an existing part (the Upper House).

It is true that the wider implications of s. 5 were not present to the minds of the law officers on the basis of whose advice the Colonial Laws Validity Act was drawn up. That advice was directed to two specific manner and form requirements: reservation of bills for the royal assent and passage of bills with certain majorities in both or either of the Houses of the legislature.[88] The rules relating to reservation are now embodied in the Australian States Constitution Act. The position, as we have seen, is that subject to certain exceptions[89] three classes of bills must be reserved: (1) bills altering the constitution of the legislature or either House thereof, (2) bills affecting the salary of the Governor of the State, (3) bills requiring to be reserved by State legislation passed after 1907.[90] Reserved bills which are assented to do not have force until the Governor signifies that royal assent has been given.[91] While the Australian States Constitution Act states that nothing in the Act is to affect the reservation of bills in accordance with Instructions given by the monarch to the Governor,[92] the effect of s. 4 of the Colonial Laws Validity Act is that a failure to reserve such bills does not invalidate them. However, failure to reserve a bill falling

---

[88]See Blackmore, *The South Australian Constitution*, pp.64-67.

[89]They are found in s. 1 (1), Provisos (b) and (c), of the Australian States Constitution Act (1907). It is not necessary to reserve a bill for a temporary law for which assent of the Governor is necessary by reason of some "public and pressing emergency" or a bill with respect to which the Governor has received instructions from the monarch either to assent or to refuse assent. In *Taylor's Case* the Parliamentary Bills Referendum Act (1908) of Queensland, which was impugned on the ground, *inter alia*, that it had not been reserved, was held to be valid on the ground that the Governor had received instructions to assent to it. In *Burt* v. *The Crown* (1935) 37 W.A.L.R. 68 a bill impugned on the ground of non-reservation was held to have come within Proviso (b). S. 1 (2) excludes from the operation of the Act bills which alter electoral districts or the number of members to be elected for a district or House of Parliament, or which relate to the qualifications of members or electors.

[90]S. 1 (1) (a), (b), (c).

[91]S. 1 (3); Australian Constitutions Act (1842), s. 33. Such assent is to be signified by proclamation or by message to both Houses (of the State Parliament).

[92]S. 1 (1), Proviso (a).

within one of the three classes specified in the Australian States Constitution Act would constitute non-compliance with ss. 4 and 5 of the Colonial Laws Validity Act and would render the enactment inoperative.[93]

Certain Imperial acts such as the Merchant Shipping Act contain provisions that local legislation regulating matters covered therein shall contain a clause suspending the operation of the legislation until the royal assent has been publicly signified. In *R.* v. *Commissioner for Transport ex parte Cobb & Co. Ltd.*[94] the Full Court of Queensland struck down transport legislation of the State for failure to comply with this requirement as embodied in s. 736 of the Merchant Shipping Act. The members of the Court considered that the Australian States Constitution Act had not swept away the requirement of a suspending clause contained in the Merchant Shipping Act, basing their argument on the ground that the Australian States Constitution Act referred to reservation of bills while the Merchant Shipping Act imposed a requirement of a suspending clause in acts.[95] It is submitted, however, that the difference is not a substantial one but merely one of form, that in both cases there is no operative act until the royal assent has been given, and that therefore in substance the requirement of a suspending clause amounts to a requirement of reservation. If this submission be correct, it would seem that, unless the subject matter of a bill to which the suspending clause requirement relates falls within s. 1 of the Australian States Constitution Act, a failure to include such a clause does not invalidate the legislation.[96]

On the question of legislative majorities, there are provisions in the

---

[93] See *Trethowan* v. *Attorney-General for New South Wales* (1930-31) 44 C.L.R., at p.432, per Dixon, J. See also the differing views of Isaacs, J., and Starke, J., as to the effect of non-reservation of bills passed by the Commonwealth Parliament in *John Sharp & Sons Pty. Ltd.* v. *The "Katherine Mackall"* (1924) 34 C.L.R. 420, at pp.430, 433. It is to be noted, however, that the Australian States Constitution Act does not apply to Commonwealth Acts.

[94] [1963] Qd.R. 547.

[95] *Ibid.*, at pp.560-61 (Mansfield, C.J.); pp.568-70 (Stanley, J., expressing some doubt, however); pp.583-87 (Wanstall, J.).

[96] See, however, B. A. Helmore, "Validity of State Navigation Acts", 27 *Australian Law Journal* (1953-54), 16. Two further points may be noted about *Cobb's Case*. In the first place the majority considered that the State legislation was invalid on the ground of repugnancy whereas, as Wanstall, J., pointed out, the alleged incompatibility suggested a question of manner and form rather than repugnancy. See his argument at pp.585-86. In the second place, the transport act of the State which was struck down dealt mainly with road transport and contained only a few clauses dealing with sea transport. Nevertheless, the Court held that there could be no severance of the invalid from the valid portions. But see the decision of the Privy Council in *Bribery Commissioner* v. *Ranasinghe* [1964] 2 W.L.R. 1301, at p.1313.

South Australian,[97] Victorian,[98] and Western Australian[99] Constitution Acts which require absolute majorities for bills altering the constitutions of the Houses of the legislatures.[100] The requirement of certain types of majorities which was originally part of the Constitution of New South Wales was repealed. It seems clear that these requirements can be repealed by a simple majority in both Houses of a State Parliament, as no requirement is to be found in the original Acts which specify that the provisions as to majorities can only be repealed by the same majorities.[102] However, the repeal of such majorities provisions must be express insofar as until repealed they operate as manner and form requirements under s. 5 and therefore bind future Parliaments. As we shall see later, the right to challenge legislation which does not comply with this particular manner and form requirement is attended by certain difficulties.[103]

The requirement of a referendum is one to which State Parliaments have had recourse to entrench the status of the Legislative Council. It is to be found as we have seen in ss. 7A and 5B of the New South Wales Constitution Act. It is also to be found in s. 24A of that Act which prohibits the life of the Assembly from being extended beyond three years unless the extending act is approved at a referendum. Such a provision fettering the power of Parliament to extend its life is also to be found in the Queensland Constitution[104] which also prohibits the reintroduction of an Upper House without a referendum.[105] The South Australian Constitution Act Amendment Act of 1969 has imposed the requirement in relation to bills affecting a number of matters including bills abolishing *either* the Assembly *or* the Council.[105] A further

[97]C.A. (S.A.), ss.8, 41. See also C.A. Amendment Act (1969).
[98]C.A. (Vic.), s. 18. See also C.A. (Vic.), ss.67, 68.
[99]C.A. (W.A.), s. 73.
[100]There is authority for the proposition that a bill altering electoral districts is not a bill altering the constitution of the legislature or either House thereof: *McDonald* v. *Cain* (1953) 60 A.L.R. 965, at pp. 993-94. See also *Kenny* v. *Chapman* (1861) 1 W. & W. (L.) 93; *Clydesdale* v. *Hughes* (1934) 51 C.L.R. 518.
[101]See Act No. 79 of 1972, s. 3.
[102]This is clear, for example, from s. 4 of the New South Wales Constitution Statute and sections of the Constitution Acts of the other States which conferred power of constitutional alteration, and also from the opinion of the Secretary of State for the Colonies in a despatch to the Governor of New South Wales explaining the Constitution Act (*New South Wales Legislative Council Votes and Proceedings*, Vol. I, 1855), that these provisions could be modified in the ordinary manner. Both the New South Wales and Queensland majorities provisions were repealed by legislation passed with ordinary majorities.
[103]Pp.104 *et seq.*
[104]Constitution Act Amendment Act (1934), s. 3.
[105]*Ibid.,* s. 4.

amendment act of 1975 (No. 122) has extended the requirement to legislation affecting rules relating to electoral redistribution inserted by the amending act into the South Australian Constitution.

However, difficulties have arisen when it comes to the question of determining the right of an individual citizen to take action in the courts to restrain a government from acting contrary to these manner and form requirements. At the outset the plaintiff in such an action must show a sufficient interest to support his claim in declaration or injunction proceedings. This vital question, although it had been argued before the New South Wales Supreme Court in *Trethowan's Case* and decided in favour of the plaintiffs,[107] was excluded from the issues before the High Court[108] and Privy Council in that case. In *McDonald* v. *Cain*,[109] where an action was brought for a declaration that a bill altering electoral districts was subject to the requirement under the Victorian Constitution Act that it be passed with an absolute majority in the Legislative Council, the Victorian Full Court, while rejecting the argument that such a bill was subject to the majorities provision, considered that the plaintiffs had a sufficient interest as voters and also as members of the legislature to take such proceedings.[110] This view was approved by the Western Australian Full Court in *Tonkin* v. *Brand*,[111] but in *Clayton* v. *Heffron* the High Court cast doubt on the *locus standi* of the plaintiffs, the majority of whom were members of the House which the bill in question was designed to abolish, and suggested that the interest of the plaintiffs as members of the Council or as taxpayers[112] did not confer *locus standi*.[113]

Even, however, if this preliminary obstacle is overcome by the plain-

---

[106]S. 10(a) added by s. 2.

[107](1931) 31 S.R. (N.S.W.) 183, at pp.204-6, 219, 232-33.

[108](1930-31) 44 C.L.R., at pp.399-400.

[109](1953) 60 A.L.R. 965.

[110]*Ibid.*, at pp.972, 978, 988.

[111][1962] W.A.R. 1, at pp.14-15, 19, 21. However, the majority of the Court did not decide the question whether the interest of the plaintiffs as members of parliament was sufficient, preferring to base their judgment on the ground that their interest as voters was sufficient.

[112]Who, it was alleged, were prejudicially affected by the proposed expenditure of money on a referendum which was claimed not to be sanctioned by the New South Wales Constitution.

[113](1960-61) 105 C.L.R., at p.233. The Court did not discuss the question whether the right to vote constituted a sufficient interest. In *Cormack* v. *Cope* [1974] 48 A.L.J.R. 319 at 324-25, Barwick, C.J. considered that a member of the Senate had *locus standi* in proceedings involving the joint sitting procedure under s. 57 of the Commonwealth Constitution.

tiff he is faced with the task of convincing the court that relief by way of an injunction or declaration should be granted either at a preliminary stage before the impugned bill receives the royal assent or, at a later stage, after that assent is given. In *McDonald* v. *Cain*[114] and *Tonkin* v. *Brand*[115] it was recognized that relief by way of declaration was within the jurisdiction of the court. It must be noted, however, that there is a traditional constitutional principle which prevents the courts from reviewing matters of internal parliamentary procedure unless they are authorized to do so. Such matters are regarded as being within the sole cognizance of the legislature.[116] It seems clear from *Clayton* v. *Heffron* that at least an injunction would not be granted by a court to restrain ministers from taking steps to submit a bill to a referendum according to the procedure laid down in s. 5B of the New South Wales Constitution Act.[117] *A fortiori* it would seem that the type of relief sought in *Trethowan's Case*, the granting of an injunction to restrain presentation of a bill for the royal assent (a question not discussed by the higher courts in that case), would not have been sanctioned by the High Court in *Clayton* v. *Heffron* if it had been in issue.[118] Such matters, it can be said, fall within the broad concept of parliamentary procedure which is not confined merely to the passage of the bill through the Houses, but extends to subsequent acts leading up to the assent of the Governor to the bill. If this is so, it could be suggested that the grant of the remedy of a declaration at the preliminary stage, although not followed by any coercive relief, might constitute an interference by the courts with the parliamentary process.[119]

The attitude of the High Court to judicial intervention in the legislative process which was expressed in *Clayton* v. *Heffron* has been affected by dicta in the recent case of *Cormack* v. *Cope*[120] which in-

---

[114](1953) 60 A.L.R., at pp.977-78, 987-88. Gavan Duffy, J., did not decide the point.

[115][1962] W.A.R. 1, at pp.15-16, 19-20, 21-22. In this case, the relief sought was to determine whether ministers of the Crown were under an obligation to tender certain advice to the Governor.

[116]See *Bradlaugh* v. *Gossett* (1884) 12 Q.B.D. 271. *Edinburgh & Dalkeith Railway Co.* v. *Wauchope* (1842) 8 C. & F. 710. *R.* v. *Richards, Ex parte Fitzpatrick & Browne* (1954-55) 92 C.L.R. 157.

[117]105 C.L.R., at pp. 233-35.

[118]In *Hughes & Vale Ltd.* v. *Gair* (1954) 90 C.L.R. 203 doubt was cast on the availability of the remedy although it was pointed out that in *Trethowan's Case* there was a statutory prohibition against submitting for the royal assent a bill which had not been approved at a referendum. Of course no compulsive remedy is available against the Governor *R.* v. *Governor of South Australia* (1907) 4 C.L.R. 1497.

[119]But see Enid Campbell, *Parliamentary Privilege in Australia* (Melbourne: Melbourne University Press, 1966), p.89.

[120](1974) 48 A.L.J.R. 319.

volved a challenge to procedures taken by the Commonwealth Government to have six Bills debated and passed at a joint sitting of both Houses of the Federal Parliament held under s. 57 of the Commonwealth Constitution. The members of the Court in this case commented on the jurisdiction of the Court to intervene to adjudicate on the validity of the procedure followed with respect to the Bills before they had been presented for the royal assent. The Privy Council decision in *Rediffusion (Hong Kong) Ltd.* v. *Attorney-General of Hong Kong*[121] where such jurisdiction was recognized in respect of intervention in the processes of the legislature of a Crown Colony was referred to. Two judges (Barwick, C. J. and Gibbs, J.) favoured the view that the Court had the right to intervene in the legislative process.[122] Mc-Tiernan, J. rejected this view. Menzies and Stephen, J. J. considered that such intervention would be proper only in cases (if there were any) in which the jurisdiction to deal effectively with the legislation when enacted would be defeated.[123] The Court refused the application for the injunction on the basis that the validity of the procedure could be examined after the Bills became law.

Relief at a subsequent stage—after the bill has received royal assent—may be granted to a plaintiff who can show that his interests have been infringed. This distinction between relief at a preliminary stage and a relief at a subsequent stage is brought out strongly in a passage of the majority judgment in *Clayton* v. *Heffron*:

> ... The Court in acting upon the concession[124] must go beyond its function of deciding whether an Act of Parliament assented to by the Crown does not go beyond the legislative power of the Parliament so that it cannot form part of the law of the land and must enter upon an enquiry into the lawfulness and regularity of the course pursued within the Parliament itself in the process of legislation and before its completion. It is an enquiry which according to the traditional view courts do not undertake. The process of lawmaking is one thing, the power to make the law as it emerged from the process is another. *It is the latter which the court must always have jurisdiction to examine and pronounce upon.* Of course the framers of a constitution may make the validity of any law dependent upon any fact, event or consideration they may choose and, if one is chosen which consists in a proceeding in Parliament, the

---

[121] [1970] A.C. 1136.
[122] 48 A.L.J.R. at 322, 327.
[123] *Ibid.*, at 327, 330.
[124] I.e. the concession of the defendants to submit to the jurisdiction of the Court so that the constitutional question could be decided.

courts must take it under their cognizance in order to determine whether the supposed law is a valid law; but even then one might suppose only after the law in question has been enacted and when its validity as law is impugned by someone affected by its operation.[125]

It would seem therefore, as Professor Sawer has suggested,[126] that in any legislation which imposes manner and form provisions an express provision authorizing the citizen to seek relief by way of injunction proceedings might be required before the courts could take jurisdiction at the preliminary stage. In the absence of such a clause, the courts may decline to intervene.[127] However, this does not mean that no remedy is available to prevent the unconstitutional passage of such a bill. It would seem that this may be a proper case for the Governor of the State to withhold assent to the bill on the ground that the proper manner and form for the passage of legislation has not been observed.[128]

At a subsequent stage, however, legal remedies would be available to a citizen who could show that his interests were affected by the legislation. But even at this stage the court may be debarred from enquiring into manner and form requirements which pertain to the relationship between the Houses and the mode of passage of a bill unless such provisions are held to be imperative and requisite to the validity of the bill. The law officers in their opinion preceding the enactment of the Colonial Laws Validity Act seemed to hold this view at least in respect to absolute majority provisions. An authenticated act of Parliament would not necessarily indicate the procedure which had preceded the enactment of a bill,[129] and s. 6 of the Colonial Laws Validity Act provides that the authenticated act is to be taken as prima facie evidence that the act has been passed in the proper manner and

[125] 105 C.L.R., at pp.234-35. My italics.
[126] "Injunction, Parliamentary Process and the Restriction of Parliamentary Competence", 60 *Law Quarterly Review* (1944), 86.
[127] S. 10(a) (7) of the South Australian Constitution Act provides that a person entitled to vote shall have the right to bring action for equitable relief either *before* or after royal assent has been given to a bill subject to a manner and form requirement. See also s. 88 (5) inserted by C.A. Amendment Act No. 122 of 1975.
[128] See pp.98 *et seq.* Of course, the Speaker would also be in a position to give a ruling on such a bill and to declare it lapsed if it failed to attain the required majority. This happened in South Australia in 1964, when the Speaker (an Independent) declared that a bill altering the constitution of the Houses which did not obtain an absolute majority *ipso facto* lapsed. See 10 *Australian Journal of Politics and History* (1964), 236-38.
[129] Blackmore, *The South Australian Constitution*, pp.67-69. However, the law officers seemed to envisage that the question might be raised by the adduction of "proper" evidence from outside the copy of the act itself.

form.[130] It appears, however, from the recent decision of the Judicial Committee in *Bribery Commissioner* v. *Ranasinghe*[131] that an act may impose a requirement that a later amending act be authenticated with a certificate of the Speaker that the (later) act has been passed with the required majority of members. Such a certificate will be regarded as an essential part of the legislative process necessary for amending the earlier act. In *Clayton* v. *Heffron* the majority of the Court regarded the procedures laid down in s. 5B of the New South Wales Constitution Act as to the free conference between managers of the Houses and the joint sitting as directory and not mandatory provisions, failure to comply with which did not entail invalidity.[132] However, the courts would always be entitled and indeed obliged to determine whether a bill had been passed by both Houses, for otherwise, subject of course to deadlock provisions where they exist, it would not be an act of Parliament but merely a resolution of one House.[133] On the other hand a provision laying down a manner and form procedure which involves the approval of a bill by the electors voting at a referendum would be subject to judicial review in invalidity proceedings brought after royal assent has been given to the bill. In this case failure to comply with the requirement would be apparent on the face of the act or could be proved by other appropriate evidence, and the requirement would be regarded as mandatory—a condition precedent to the validity of a bill falling within the prescribed procedure.

In *State of Victoria* v. *Commonwealth of Australia*[134] the High

---

[130]It might be suggested that the official parliamentary debates of the State could be put in evidence to rebut the presumption of the validity of the act authenticated by the certificate of the Clerk of Parliament, but see D. V. Cowen, "Legislature and Judiciary: Reflections on the Constitutional Issues in South Africa", 16 *Modern Law Review* (1953), 277.

[131][1964] 2 W.L.R. 1301.

[132]However, in *Harris* v. *Donges* [1952] 1 T.L.R. 1245, discussed in G. Marshall, *Parliamentary Sovereignty and the Commonwealth* (Oxford: Clarendon Press, 1957), pp.170 *et seq.*, the Appellate Division of the South African Supreme Court regarded a provision for a joint sitting as a mandatory provision. In that case the South Africa Act (1909) had prescribed that legislation of a certain nature must be passed at a joint sitting of both Houses of Parliament. But the joint sitting in *Clayton* v. *Heffron* was not of this nature: it was a joint sitting for *discussion* on the bill. However, the joint sitting provided for in the Victorian Constitution is a joint sitting for the *enactment* of a bill which is subject to deadlock and on the authority of *Harris* v. *Donges* would probably be regarded as mandatory and within judicial cognizance, if proper evidence were available of non-compliance with the requirement. In *McDonald* v. *Cain* the Victorian Full Court took the view that a requirement of absolute majorities in the Victorian Constitution Act entitled it to determine whether a bill had been passed with such majorities: (1953) 60 A.L.R., at pp.970-971, 977, 984-85.

[133]See *Stevenson* v. *R.* (1865) 2 W.W. & A.B. (L.) 143.

[134](1975) 7 A.L.R. 1.

Court was concerned with a challenge to one of the Bills passed at a joint sitting of the Federal Parliament held under s. 57 of the Commonwealth Constitution, one of the grounds being that the Senate had not "failed to pass" the Bill when it took certain action with regard to it on a particular day. The Court held that it had jurisdiction to determine whether the Upper House action amounted to a failure to pass and that the requirement that a certain interval elapse before re-presentation of the Bill to the Lower House was mandatory. This would suggest that similar provisions in State Constitutions would also be regarded as mandatory.[135]

MANNER AND FORM REQUIREMENTS OUTSIDE THE COLONIAL LAWS VALIDITY ACT

Our previous discussion has centred around the effect of manner and form provisions on subsequent legislation relating to the constitution, powers or procedure of a State legislature, and it has been argued that it is only such legislation which falls within s. 5 of the Colonial Laws Validity Act. It remains to be considered whether there exists any power outside the Colonial Laws Validity Act for a State legislature to impose manner and form requirements on future legislation which does not come within this category. In *McCawley* v. *The King*[136] the Judicial Committee of the Privy Council, in holding that a provision of the Queensland Constitution Act could be impliedly amended by a later act passed in the ordinary manner, emphasized the flexible nature of the Constitutions of the States and contrasted them with controlled or rigid constitutions.[137] However, as we have seen rigidity can be introduced into the Constitutions of the States by recourse to s. 5 of the Colonial Laws Validity Act. Moreover, with respect to other types of legislation the reasoning of the High Court in *Clayton* v. *Heffron* supports the view that in respect of legislation falling within a general or particular category the constituent parts of a legislature can be modified. S. 5A of the New South Wales Constitution Act has this effect in relation to appropriation bills.[138] The assent of the Upper House is effectively dispensed with so that with regard to this class of legislation the legislature consists of two component parts

---

[135][1920] A.C. 691.

[136]I.e. those provisions relating to actions by the Upper House in relation to bills which are the subject of deadlock.

[137]*Ibid.*, at pp.703-6. The Judicial Committee did recognize, however, that a special amending process could be introduced in certain cases (at p.714).

[138]See p.52.

only: the Crown and the Legislative Assembly. With regard to all other types of bills the structure of the New South Wales legislature is also modified: the Legislative Council may delay the passage of a bill but in the words of the majority judgment in *Clayton* v. *Heffron* "the power to legislate ... may be exercised by the Crown with the consent of the Assembly provided the proposed law is approved by the majority of electors voting at a referendum".[139]

The power to enact legislation modifying the constituent parts of the legislature was considered by the High Court to be derived from the section of the New South Wales Constitution Act (existing in a similar form in the Constitution Acts of the other States) which empowers the legislature to make laws for the peace, order, and good government of the State in all cases whatsoever. Such an alteration of the component parts of the legislature would be applicable to ordinary as well as to constitutional legislation.[140] The proposition that a legislature, quite apart from the provisions of the Colonial Laws Validity Act, can change its structure is also supported by the South African case of *Harris* v. *Donges*.[141] The proposition means that a legislature, instead of continuing to function in the ordinary manner, that is to say, by enacting legislation which has the assent of the two Houses and the Crown, may modify its structure so as to augment or diminish its component parts for future legislation and therefore change its manner and form of legislating. Although it has been argued by some writers that such a doctrine is inapplicable to the United Kingdom Parliament on the ground that it contravenes the principle of parliamentary supremacy,[142] it is pointed out by others that it applies to all legislatures irrespective of their origin, whether in common law or statute, and that it does not in fact infringe the principle of parliamentary supremacy: Parliament still retains its legislative power but the structure of Parliament in exercising that power is modified.[143]

---

[139] 105 C.L.R., at p.252.
[140] *Ibid.*, at p.250. See also the judgment of Menzies, J., at p.275. *Commonwealth Aluminium Corporation Ltd.* v. *Attorney-General for Queensland* (1974, as yet unreported, dissenting judgment of Hoare J.).
[141] [1952] 1 T.L.R. 1245.
[142] H. W. R. Wade, "The Basis of Legal Sovereignty", *Cambridge Law Journal* (1955), 172.
[143] See D. V. Cowen, "Legislature and Judiciary: Reflections on the Constitutional Issues in South Africa", 15 *Modern Law Review* (1952), 282, 16 *Modern Law Review* (1953), 273, and *Parliamentary Sovereignty and the Entrenched Provisions of the South Africa Act* (1951); R. V. Heuston, *Principles of Constitutional Law* (London: Stevens & Sons, 1961), chap. 1; Marshall, *Parliamentary Sovereignty and the Commonwealth,* especially chap. 4; W. Friedmann, "Trethowan's Case,

It would seem, however, that a State legislature cannot modify the prerogative of the Governor to assent to bills or abolish the Crown by making the constitution of the State a republican one.[144] It can therefore be argued that under the powers conferred by the Constitution Acts to make laws the various State legislatures can introduce fetters into their legislative structure which will control not only constitutional legislation falling outside s. 5 of the Colonial Laws Validity Act but also ordinary legislation.[145] It is under this power that a Bill of Rights could be introduced into the Constitution of a State and could be entrenched by requiring a referendum for its modification or repeal.[146] The effect of such a change would be that for the purpose of legislating in the area covered by the Bill of Rights the legislature would assume a different structure: it would consist of the Crown, the two Houses (in Queensland, one House) and the electorate voting at a referendum. In effect, therefore, s. 5 of the Colonial Laws Validity Act is merely an application of this doctrine to a particular class of legislation: legislation concerning the constitution, powers or procedure of the legislature. However, it must also be remembered that the entrenching section—the section which provides for a different method of legislating for the particular type of legislation covered by it—must itself be entrenched before it will effectively bind a later Parliament,

---

Parliamentary Sovereignty and the Limits of Legal Change", 24 *Australian Law Journal* (1951), 103. See also Fajgenbaum and Hanks, *Australian Constitutional Law*, pp.263-66.

[144]This was the basis of the rejection by the Imperial authorities of several of the original Constitution Acts of the Australian colonies which purported to fetter the prerogative of the Governor in respect of his assent to bills. See also *Taylor* v. *Attorney-General for Queensland* (1916-17) 23 C.L.R., at pp.474, 481; *Clayton* v. *Heffron* 105 C.L.R., at p.251; and the Tasmanian case of *Re Scully* (1937) 32 Tas. L.R. 1, especially at pp.42 *et seq.* where Clark, J., pointed out that the elimination of the Crown would infringe s. 31 of the Australian Constitutions Act (1842) which requires bills passed by the legislature to be submitted to the Governor for the Queen's assent. He also considered that the power of legislating could not be conferred on the Governor acting alone: 32 Tas L.R., at p.35. The members of the High Court in *Taylor's Case* considered that the representative character of the legislature could not be eliminated: 23 C.L.R., at pp.468, 474, 478, 481.

[145]It could be argued that there is a difference between constitutional and other types of legislation. However, subject to the qualification to be mentioned later, there does not seem to be any fundamental reason for distinguishing in this context general or specific legislation, or constitutional or non-constitutional legislation. The legislature, by prescribing a particular procedure for amendment of ordinary legislation, must be taken to have "elevated" this class of legislation to the constitutional level. In *Re Scully* (1937) 32 Tas. L.R. 1, at p.35, Clark, J., considered that a modification of the parliamentary structure for particular subjects of legislation was possible.

[146]There is a provision in the Tasmanian Constitution Act which protects freedom of religion (s. 46).

that is to say, it must be provided that the entrenching section itself can only be repealed by the same procedure; otherwise the entrenching section could be expressly repealed by an act of Parliament passed in the ordinary manner.[147]

The statement, therefore, that the Constitutions of the States are flexible, does not adequately describe the powers of a State legislature. The power of introducing rigidity into these constitutions is of course subject to abuse on the part of the members of a legislature who might desire to sanctify the status quo,[148] but it would be within the power of a court, faced with a manner and form provision which rendered it virtually impossible to repeal an act on the statute book, as for example by requiring that the repealing bill be approved by ninety per cent of electors voting at a referendum, to invalidate such legislation as fettering a State Parliament in the exercise of its powers of legislating for the peace, welfare, and good government of the State.[149] Such a provision would not merely have the effect of modifying the constituent parts of the legislature: it would be designed to abrogate the law-making power of the State legislature. It is this type of provision which would infringe the principle of parliamentary supremacy. Consequently the following qualification attaches to the power of the State Parliament to introduce rigidity into its constitution: it cannot make legislation unrepealable or impose a burdensome manner and form provision which in effect amounts to a prohibition of repeal.[150]

---

[147] The difference between what may be called a single entrenchment (which may be repealed in the ordinary way) and a double entrenchment (which cannot be repealed in the ordinary way) is illustrated by the following example.
 1 "The rights to [life, liberty, security of the person and enjoyment of property] are hereby declared to be part of the law of the State."
 2 "A bill which purports to abrogate these rights is void unless it is passed by both Houses and approved by a majority of electors voting at a referendum on the bill."
This latter provision can itself be repealed by legislation in the ordinary manner. However, a third clause may be added to secure double entrenchment.
 3 "A bill which purports to amend this section is void unless it is passed by both Houses and approved by a majority of electors voting at a referendum on the bill."
[148] In *Trethowan's Case* McTiernan, J., in a dissenting judgment ((1930-31) 44 C.L.R., at pp.433-50) viewed the referendum procedure in this light.
[149] See Friedmann, "Trethowan's Case, Parliamentary Sovereignty and the Limits of Legal Change", pp.105-6.
[150] See *Ex parte Pennington* (1875) 13 S.C.R. (N.S.W.) (L.) 305, at p.316, per Martin, C.J.

JUDICIAL REVIEW

The recognition that a State Parliament (and Executive) may be made subject to the overall control of a rigid constitution means that a judicial body will have the jurisdiction to interpret such a constitution and to pass judgment on the validity of legislative and executive action. It might be argued that the Supreme Courts of the States, the bulk of the jurisdiction of which consists of common law matters, are not appropriate organs for the upholding and enforcement of constitutional rules. But an examination of the historical development of the colonial constitutions shows that the judges of the Supreme Courts were intended even in the era before responsible government to exercise the power of judicial review of legislative acts. That they continued to exercise such a jurisdiction (although not specifically granted by the Constitution Acts) after the advent of responsible government, which brought with it a greater security of tenure, is clear. Such a jurisdiction is necessarily inherent in the courts of a system which has a controlled constitution.[151] The Supreme Courts of the States would be not merely fulfilling a historic function but also a function in accord with comparative constitutional practice (cf. the Supreme Courts of the American States), by participating in judicial exegesis and application of constitutional rules. The provisions of the Constitution Acts governing the appointment[152] and dismissal[153] of Supreme Court judges confer on them a security of tenure which is essential for the performance of their duties, and which protects them from executive interference. They would therefore have a status which would enable them to assume an effective role as guardians of a State Constitution which imposes fetters on the exercise of legislative and executive power.

---

[151] The Victorian Constitution Act of 1975, s. 85(1), expressly confers a jurisdiction "in or in relation to Victoria, its dependencies and the areas adjacent thereto in all cases whatsoever ... ".

[152] The appointment is during good behaviour, the traditional method of guaranteeing the tenure of superior court judges, following the pattern of the *Act of Settlement* 1701. This tenure is subject to a retiring age. See Fajgenbaum and Hanks, *Australian Constitutional Law*, chap. 14.

[153] See p.73.

[154] See generally Z. Cowen and D. P. Derham, "The Independence of Judges", 26 *Australian Law Journal* (1952-53), 462; "The Constitutional Position of Judges", 29 *Australian Law Journal* (1956), 705. However, the position of the judges is not constitutionally *entrenched* for the first paragraph of s. 5 of the Colonial Laws Validity Act allows the legislature to modify the judicial structure. In *Clyne* v. *East* [1967] 2 N.S.W.R. 483, it was held that the doctrine of the separation of powers does not form part of the constitutional structure of the States.

CONCLUSION

The preceding discussion has shown that the legislative power of the Australian States is subject to certain limitations under the Colonial Laws Validity Act, first in regard to the power to enact legislation repugnant to British legislation which extends to the States, secondly in the requirement that certain classes of bills be reserved for the royal assent, and thirdly in the requirement that laws respecting the constitution, powers, or procedure of the legislature must be passed in the manner and form laid down by existing law. However, this third requirement, we have argued, exists quite independently of the Colonial Laws Validity Act and is not restricted to laws of the nature specified therein. The fourth type of limitation on the legislative power of the States arises from the territorial limitation which has been interpreted by the courts as being implicit in the grant of power to make laws for the peace, order (welfare), and good government of the State.[155]

It is clear that the time is ripe for the repeal of the Colonial Laws Validity Act in respect of the Australian States and for the extension to them of the "autonomy" provisions of the Statute of Westminster,[156] so as to give them full legislative power commensurate with their responsibilities as component parts of the Commonwealth of Australia.[157] It may be objected that the removal of the territorial limitation—if such a limitation does survive[158]—would lead to difficulties in reconciling the legislative jurisdiction of the States *inter se*, for example in respect of taxing legislation, but the possibility of clashes between State statutes could be averted if a federal conflicts doctrine were worked out to control the statutes of one State which operate on persons, acts, or events in another State.[159]

---

[155] See, however, F. A. Trindade, "The Australian States and the Doctrine of Extraterritorial Legislative Competence", 45 A.L.J. (1971) 233 at 240-41.

[156] Under s. 2 of the Statute it was provided that the Colonial Laws Validity Act should not apply after the commencement of the Act (in Australia this was 1939) to a law of the Parliament of the Dominion. No act of that Parliament was to be invalid on the ground that it was repugnant to British legislation and such legislation could be repealed by that Parliament. S. 3 provided that such a Parliament should have full power of making laws having extraterritorial legislation. For a disucssion of the effect of the Statute in the Australian federal system see Bailey, "The Statute of Westminster", pp.362, 398. K. C. Wheare, *The Statute of Westminister and Dominion Status* (5th ed.; London: Oxford University Press, 1953), chap. 8.

[157] When the Statute of Westminster was being drafted, the States were remiss in not requesting the application of s. 2 to themselves as did the Provinces of Canada. See comment by Sir Robert Garran in 13 *British Year Book of International Law* (1932), 116.

[158] See pp.82 *et seq.*

[159] See Castles, "Limitations on the Autonomy of the Australian States", [1962] *Public Law*, 175 at 199.

The further objection could be made that the British legislation of paramount force which applies to the States is restricted to a small number of important acts which concern the States as a whole; if the power to repeal such legislation were given to individual States, each State would be free to follow its own path and this would affect the uniformity of the present law. It would be appropriate, therefore, that uniform provisions in relation to these matters be agreed upon by the States. The effect of extending the "autonomy" provisions of the Statute of Westminster to the States would be to subject the States merely to the superior control of their own State Constitutions and the Commonwealth Constitution. It would then be a matter for the States to decide whether to overhaul their Constitutions and modernize many of the archaic provisions which are a legacy of the nineteenth century.[160] Perhaps the best method of achieving such a revision would be by the enactment of legislation providing for State constitutional conventions to be called so that exhaustive non-partisan reviews of the present Constitutions could be attempted.

[160]The Victorian Parliament has recently overhauled the Victorian Constitution. See Constitution Act (No. 8750 of 1975).

Appendices

THE COLONIAL LAWS VALIDITY ACT, 1865

(28 & 29 Vict., c.63 (Imp.))

An Act to remove Doubts as to the Validity of Colonial Laws.

Whereas Doubts have been entertained respecting the Validity of divers Laws enacted or purporting to have been enacted by the Legislatures of Certain of Her Majesty's Colonies, and respecting the Powers of such Legislatures, and it is expedient that such Doubts should be removed:

Be it hereby enacted by the Queen's most Excellent Majesty, by and with the Advice and Consent of the Lords Spiritual and Temporal, and Commons, in this present Parliament assembled, and by the Authority of the same, as follows:

1. The Term 'Colony' shall in this Act include all of Her Majesty's Possessions abroad in which there shall exist a Legislature, as hereinafter defined, except the Channel Islands, the *Isle of Man*, and such Territories as may for the Time being be vested in Her Majesty under or by virtue of any Act of Parliament for the Government of *India*:

The Terms 'Legislature' and 'Colonial Legislature' shall severally signify the Authority, other than the Imperial Parliament or Her Majesty in Council, competent to make Laws for any Colony:

The Term 'Representative Legislature' shall signify any Colonial Legislature which shall comprise a Legislative Body of which One Half are elected by Inhabitants of the Colony:

The Term 'Colonial Law' shall include Laws made for any Colony either by such Legislature as aforesaid or by Her Majesty in Council:

An Act of Parliament, or any Provision thereof, shall, in construing this Act, be said to extend to any Colony when it is made applicable to such Colony by the express Words or necessary Intendment of any Act of Parliament:

The Term 'Governor' shall mean the Officer lawfully administering the Government of any Colony:

The Term 'Letters Patent' shall mean Letters Patent under the Great Seal of the United Kingdom of *Great Britain* and *Ireland*.

2. Any Colonial Law which is or shall be in any respect repugnant to the Provisions of any Act of Parliament extending to the Colony to which such Law may relate, or repugnant to any Order or Regulation made under Authority of such Act of Parliament, or having in the Colony the Force and Effect of such Act, shall be read subject to such Act, Order or Regulation, and shall, to the Extent of such Repugnancy, but not otherwise, be and remain absolutely void and inoperative.

3. No Colonial Law shall be or be deemed to have been void or inoperative on the Ground of Repugnancy to the Law of *England*, unless the

same shall be repugnant to the Provisions of some such Act of Parliament, Order or Regulation as aforesaid.

4. No Colonial Law, passed with the Concurrence of or assented to by the Governor of any Colony, or to be here-after so passed or assented to, shall be or be deemed to have been void or inoperative by reason only of any Instructions with reference to such Law or the Subject thereof which may have been given to such Governor by or on behalf of Her Majesty, by any Instrument other than the Letters Patent or Instrument authorising such Governor to concur in passing or to assent to Laws for the Peace, Order, and good Government of such Colony, even though such Instructions may be referred to in such Letters Patent or last-mentioned Instrument.

5. Every Colonial Legislature shall have, and be deemed at all Times to have had, full Power within its Jurisdiction to establish Courts of Judicature, and to abolish and reconstitute the same, and to alter the Constitution thereof, and to make Provision for the Administration of Justice therein; and every Representative Legislature shall, in respect to the Colony under its Jurisdiction, have, and be deemed at all Times to have had, full Power to make Laws respecting the Constitution, Powers, and Procedure of such Legislature; provided that such Laws shall have been passed in such Manner and Form as may from Time to Time be required by any Act of Parliament, Letters Patent, Order in Council, or Colonial Law for the Time being in force in the said Colony.

6. The Certificate of the Clerk or other proper Officer of a Legislative Body in any Colony to the Effect that the Document to which it is attached is a true Copy of any Colonial Law assented to by the Governor of such Colony, or ,of any Bill reserved for the Signification of Her Majesty's Pleasure by the said Governor, shall be *prima facie* Evidence that the Document so certified is a true Copy of such Law or Bill, and, as the Case may be, that such Law has been duly and properly passed and presented to the Governor; and any Proclamation purporting to be published by Authority of the Governor in any Newspaper in the Colony to which such Law or Bill shall relate, and signifying Her Majesty's Disallowance of any such Colonial Law, or Her Majesty's Assent to any such reserved Bill as aforesaid, shall be *prima facie* Evidence of such Disallowance or Assent.

And whereas Doubts are entertained respecting the Validity of certain Acts enacted or reputed to be enacted by the Legislature of *South Australia*: Be it further enacted as follows:

7. All Laws or reputed Laws enacted or purporting to have been enacted by the said Legislature, or by Persons or Bodies of Persons for the Time being acting as such Legislature, which have received the Assent of Her Majesty in Council, or which have received the Assent of the Governor of the said Colony in the Name and on behalf of Her Majesty, shall be and be deemed to have been valid and effectual from the Date of such Assent for all Purposes whatever; provided that nothing herein contained shall be deemed to give Effect to any Law or reputed Law which has been disallowed by Her Majesty, or has expired, or has been lawfully repealed, or to prevent the lawful Disallowance or Repeal of any Law.

AUSTRALIAN STATES
CONSTITUTION ACT, 1907

(7 Edw. VII, c.7 (Imp.))

An Act to amend the Law relating to the Reservation for His Majesty's pleasure of Bills passed by the Legislatures of the States forming part of the Commonwealth of Australia, and to confirm certain Acts passed by those Legislatures.

1. (1.) There shall be reserved, for the signification of His Majesty's pleasure thereon, every Bill passed by the Legislature of any State forming part of the Commonwealth of Australia which-

(a) Alters the constitution of the Legislature of the State or of either House thereof; or

(b) Affects the salary of the Governor of the State; or

(c) Is, under any Act of the Legislature of the State passed after the passing of this Act, or under any provision contained in the Bill itself, required to be reserved;

but, save as aforesaid, it shall not be necessary to so reserve any Bill passed by any such Legislature:

Provided that-

(a) Nothing in this Act shall affect the reservation of Bills in accordance with any instructions given to the Governor of the State by His Majesty; and

(b) It shall not be necessary to reserve a Bill for a temporary law which the Governor expressly declares necessary to be assented to forthwith by reason of some public and pressing emergency; and

(c) It shall not be necessary to reserve any Bill if the Governor declares that he withholds His Majesty's assent, or if he has previously received instructions from His Majesty to assent and does assent accordingly to the Bill.

(2.) For the purposes of this section a Bill shall not be treated as a Bill altering the constitution of the Legislature of a State or of either House thereof by reason only that the Bill-

(a) Creates, alters, or affects any province, district, or town, or division of a province, district, or town, which returns one or more members to either House of the Legislature; or

(b) Fixes or alters the number of members to be elected for any such province, district, or town, or division of a province, district, or town; or

(c) Increases or decreases the total number of elective members of either House of the Legislature; or

(d) Concerns the election of the elective members of the Legislature, or either House thereof, or the qualifications of electors or elective members.

(3.) Section thirty-three of the Australian Constitutions Act, 1842, shall apply to Bills reserved under this Act in like manner as it applies to Bills reserved under that Act with the substitution of references to a State forming part of the Commonwealth of Australia for references to the colony of New South Wales, and of references to both Houses of the Legislature of the State for references to the Legislative Council.

(4.) So much of any Act of Parliament or Order in Council as requires any Bill passed by the Legislature of any such State to be reserved for the signification of His Majesty's pleasure thereon, or to be laid before the Houses of Parliament before His Majesty's pleasure is signified, and, in particular, the enactments mentioned in the Schedule to this Act, to the extent specified in the third column of that Schedule, shall be repealed both as originally enacted and as incorporated in or applied by any other Act of Parliament or any Order in Council or letters patent.

2. (1.) Any Act passed by the Legislature of any such State, and assented to in the name of His Majesty by the Governor and not disallowed by His Majesty before the passing of this Act, shall, notwithstanding that the Bill for the Act ought to have been but was not reserved for the signification of His Majesty's pleasure thereon, and notwithstanding that it ought to have been but was not duly laid before both Houses of Parliament, be deemed to be and to have been as from the date of that assent as valid as if the Bill had been so reserved and as if it had been laid before both Houses of Parliament, and as if His Majesty's assent to the Bill had been duly given and signified in the State at the date aforesaid.

(2.) For the purposes of this section references to Acts passed by the Legislature of a State shall be construed as including references to Acts passed before the establishment of the Commonwealth of Australia by the Legislature of any colony which now forms part of that Commonwealth, and references to His Majesty shall be construed as including references to Her late Majesty.

3. This Act may be cited as the Australian States Constitution Act, 1907.

APPENDIX II

SCHEDULE

ENACTMENTS REPEALED

Session and Chapter	Short Title	Extent of Repeal
5 & 6 Vict. c.76	The Australian Constitutions Act, 1842	Section thirty-one, from "and all Bills altering" to the end of the section.
7 & 8 Vict. c.74	The Australian Constitutions Act, 1844	Sections seven and eight.
13 & 14 Vict. c.59	The Australian Constitutions Act, 1850	In section twelve, the words "and the reservation of Bills for the signification of Her Majesty's pleasure thereon, and the Bills so reserved". Section thirty-two, from "Provided always" to the end of the section. Section thirty-three.
18 & 19 Vict. c.54	The New South Wales Constitution Act, 1855	In section three, the words "and the reservation of Bills for the signification of Her Majesty's pleasure thereon".
18 & 19 Vict. c.55	The Victoria Constitution Act, 1855	In section three, the words "and the reservation of Bills for the signification of Her Majesty's pleasure thereon".
25 & 26 Vict. c.11	The Australian Constitutions Act, 1862	Section two.
53 & 54 Vict. c.26	The Western Australia Constitution Act, 1890	In section two, the words "and the reservation of Bills for the signification of Her Majesty's pleasure thereon".

THE STATUTE OF WESTMINSTER, 1931

(22 Geo. V, c.4)

An Act to give effect to certain resolutions passed by Imperial Conferences held in the years 1926 and 1930.

Whereas the delegates of His Majesty's Governments in the United Kingdom, the Dominion of Canada, the Commonwealth of Australia, the Dominion of New Zealand, the Union of South Africa, the Irish Free State and Newfoundland, at Imperial Conferences holden at Westminster in the years of our Lord nineteen hundred and twenty-six and nineteen hundred and thirty did concur in making the declarations and resolutions set forth in the Reports of the said Conferences:

And whereas it is meet and proper to set out by way of preamble to this Act that, inasmuch as the Crown is the symbol of the free association of the members of the British Commonwealth of Nations, and as they are united by a common allegiance to the Crown, it would be in accord with the established constitutional position of all the members of the Commonwealth in relation to one another that any alteration in the law touching the Succession to the Throne or the Royal Style and Titles shall hereafter require the assent as well of the Parliaments of all the Dominions as of the Parliament of the United Kingdom:

And whereas it is in accord with the established constitutional position that no law hereafter made by the Parliament of the United Kingdom shall extend to any of the said Dominions as part of the law of that Dominion otherwise than at the request and with the consent of that Dominion:

And whereas it is necessary for the ratifying, confirming and establishing of certain of the said declarations and resolutions of the said Conferences that a law be made and enacted in due form by authority of the Parliament of the United Kingdom:

And whereas the Dominion of Canada, the Commonwealth of Australia, the Dominion of New Zealand, the Union of South Africa, the Irish Free State and Newfoundland have severally requested and consented to the submission of a measure to the Parliament of the United Kingdom for making such provision with regard to the matters aforesaid as is hereafter in this Act contained:

Now, therefore, be it enacted by the King's most Excellent Majesty by and with the advice and consent of the Lords Spiritual and Temporal, and Commons, in this present Parliament assembled, and by the authority of the same, as follows:-

1. In this Act the expression 'Dominion' means any of the following Dominions, that is to say, the Dominion of Canada, the Commonwealth of Australia, the Dominion of New Zealand, the Union of South Africa, the Irish Free State and Newfoundland.

2.-(1) The Colonial Laws Validity Act, 1865, shall not apply to any law made after the commencement of this Act by the Parliament of a Dominion.

(2) No law and no provision of any law made after the commencement of this Act by the Parliament of a Dominion shall be void or inoperative on the ground that it is repugnant to the law of England, or to the provisions of any existing or future Act of Parliament of the United Kingdom, or to any order, rule or regulation made under any such Act, and the powers of the Parliament of a Dominion shall include the power to repeal or amend any such Act, order, rule or regulation in so far as the same is part of the law of the Dominion.

3. It is hereby declared and enacted that the Parliament of a Dominion has full power to make laws having extraterritorial operation.

4. No Act of Parliament of the United Kingdom passed after the commencement of this Act shall extend, or be deemed to extend, to a Dominion as part of the law of that Dominion, unless it is expressly declared in that Act that that Dominion has requested, and consented to, the enactment thereof.

5. Without prejudice to the generality of the foregoing provisions of this Act, sections seven hundred and thirty-five and seven hundred and thirty-six of the Merchant Shipping Act, 1894, shall be construed as though reference therein to the Legislature of a British possession did not include reference to the Parliament of a Dominion.

6. Without prejudice to the generality of the foregoing provisions of this Act, section four of the Colonial Courts of Admiralty Act, 1890 (which requires certain laws to be reserved for the signification of His Majesty's pleasure or to contain a suspending clause), and so much of section seven of that Act as requires the approval of His Majesty in Council to any rules of Court for regulating the practice and procedure of a Colonial Court of Admiralty, shall cease to have effect in any Dominion as from the commencement of this Act.

7.-(1) Nothing in this Act shall be deemed to apply to the repeal, amendment or alteration of the British North America Acts, 1867 to 1930, or any order, rule or regulation made thereunder.

(2) The provisions of section two of this Act shall extend to laws made by any of the Provinces of Canada and to the powers of the legislatures of such Provinces.

(3) The powers conferred by this Act upon the Parliament of Canada or upon the legislatures of the Provinces shall be restricted to the enactment of laws in relation to matters within the competence of the Parliament of Canada or of any of the legislatures of the Provinces respectively.

8. Nothing in this Act shall be deemed to confer any power to repeal or alter the Constitution or the Constitution Act of the Commonwealth of Australia or the Constitution Act of the Dominion of New Zealand otherwise than in accordance with the law existing before the commencement of this Act.

9.-(1) Nothing in this Act shall be deemed to authorize the Parliament of the Commonwealth of Australia to make laws on any matter within the authority of the States of Australia, not being a matter within the authority of the Parliament or Government of the Commonwealth of Australia.

(2) Nothing in this Act shall be deemed to require the concurrence of the Parliament or Government of the Commonwealth of Australia in any law made by the Parliament of the United Kingdom with respect to any matter within the authority of the States of Australia, not being a matter within the authority of the Parliament or Government of the Commonwealth of Australia, in any case where it would have been in accordance with the constitutional practice existing before the commencement of this Act that the Parliament of the United Kingdom should make that law without such concurrence.

(3) In the application of this Act to the Commonwealth of Australia the request and consent referred to in section four shall mean the request and consent of the Parliament and Government of the Commonwealth.

10.-(1) None of the following sections of this Act, that is to say, sections two, three, four, five and six, shall extend to a Dominion to which this section applies as part of the law of that Dominion unless that section is adopted by the Parliament of the Dominion, and any Act of that Parliament adopting any section of this Act may provide that the adoption shall have effect either from the commencement of this Act or from such later date as is specified in the adopting Act.

(2) The Parliament of any such Dominion as aforesaid may at any time revoke the adoption of any section referred to in subsection (1) of this section.

(3) The Dominions to which this section applies are the Commonwealth of Australia, the Dominion of New Zealand and Newfoundland.

11. Notwithstanding anything in the Interpretation Act, 1889, the expression 'Colony', shall not, in any Act of the Parliament of the United Kingdom passed after the commencement of this Act, include a Dominion or any Province or State forming part of a Dominion.

12. This Act may be cited as the Statute of Westminster, 1931.

LETTERS PATENT CONSTITUTING THE OFFICE OF GOVERNOR

(This form is taken from the Letters Patent of 1900 constituting the Office of Governor of the State of Tasmania. The Letters Patent constituting the office in other States are similar in substance although differing in matters of detail, and there are differences in the numbering of the paragraphs.)

1. [Revokes previous Letters Patent and constitutes the office of Governor of the State.]

2. *Governor's powers and authorities.-*We do hereby authorise, empower, and command our said Governor to do and execute all things that belong to his said office, according to the tenor of these our letters patent and of such commission as may be issued to him under our sign manual and signet, and according to such instructions as may from time to time be given to him under our sign manual and signet, or by our order in our Privy Council, or by us, through one of our principal Secretaries of State, and to such laws as are now or shall hereafter be in force in the State.

3. We do also by these our letters patent declare our will and pleasure as follows:-

4. *Publication of Governor's commission; Oaths to be taken by Governor.-* Every person appointed to fill the office of Governor shall, with all due solemnity, before entering on any of the duties of his office, cause the commission appointing him to be Governor to be read and published at the seat of Government, in the presence of the Chief Justice, or some other judge of the Supreme Court of the State, and of the Members of the Executive Council thereof, which being done he shall then and there take before them the oath of allegiance, in the form provided by an Act passed in the session holden in the thirty-first and thirty-second years of our reign, intituled an Act to amend the law relating to promissory oaths; and likewise the usual oath for the due execution of the office of Governor, and for the due and impartial administration of justice, which oaths the said Chief Justice or judge is hereby required to administer.

5. *Public seal.-*The Governor shall keep and use the public seal of the State for sealing all things whatsoever that shall pass the said public seal, and until a public seal shall be provided for the State the public seal formerly used in our Colony [of Tasmania] shall be used as the public seal of the State.

6. *Executive Council, Constitution of.-*There shall be an Executive Council for the State, and the said Council shall consist of such persons as were, immediately before the coming into force of these our letters patent, Members of the Executive Council of Tasmania, or as may at any time be Members of the Executive Council of our said State in accordance with any law enacted by the legislature of the State, and of such other persons as the Governor shall from time to time, in our name and on our behalf, but subject

to any law as aforesaid, appoint under the public seal of the State to be Members of our said Executive Council for the State.

7. *Grant of lands.*-The Governor, in our name and on our behalf, may make and execute, under the said public seal, grants and dispositions of any lands which may be lawfully granted and disposed of by us within the State.

8. *Appointment of judges, justices, etc.*-The Governor may constitute and appoint, in our name and on our behalf, all such judges, commissioners, justices of the peace, and other necessary officers and Ministers of the State as may be lawfully constituted or appointed by us.

9. *Grant of pardons; Remission of sentences and fines; Political offences; Removal from State.*-When any crime or offence has been committed within the State against the laws of the State, or for which the offender may be tried therein, the Governor may as he shall see occasion, in our name and on our behalf, grant a pardon to any accomplice in such crime or offence who shall give such information as shall lead to the conviction of the principal offender, or of any one of such offenders if more than one; and further, may grant to any offender convicted in any court of the State, or before any judge, or other magistrate of the State, within the State, a pardon, either free or subject to lawful conditions, or any remission of the sentence passed on such offender, or any respite of the execution of such sentence for such period as the Governor thinks fit; and further, may remit any fines, penalties, or forfeitures due or accrued to us. Provided always that the Governor shall in no case, except where the offence has been of a political nature unaccompanied by any other grave crime, make it a condition of any pardon or remission of sentence that the offender shall absent himself or be removed from the State.

10. *Suspension or removal from office.*-The Governor may, so far as we ourselves lawfully may, upon sufficient cause to him appearing, remove from his office, or suspend from the exercise of the same, any person exercising any office or place under the State, under or by virtue of any commission or warrant granted, or which may be granted, by us, in our name or under our authority.

11. *Summoning, proroguing, or dissolving any legislative body.*-The Governor may exercise all powers lawfully belonging to us in respect of the summoning, proroguing, or dissolving any legislative body, which now is or hereafter may be established within our said State.

12. *Succession to the Government; Lieutenant-Governor; Administrator to take oaths of office before administering the Government; Duties and authorities under letters patent.*-If the Governor shall be unable to administer the Government of the State by reason of any of the following causes, namely, death, incapacity, removal, or departure from the State, our Lieutenant-Governor, or if there shall be no such officer in the State, or if

such officer be unable to administer the Government of the State by reason of any of the causes aforesaid, then such person or persons as we may appoint, under our sign manual and signet, shall, during our pleasure, administer the Government of the State, first taking the Oaths hereinbefore directed to be taken by the Governor and in the manner herein prescribed; which being done, we do hereby authorise, empower, and command our Lieutenant-Governor, and every other such Administrator as aforesaid, to do and execute during our pleasure all things that belong to the office of Governor according to the tenour of these our letters patent, and according to our instructions as aforesaid, and the laws of the State.

[This clause was substituted for previous clause 12 by letters patent of 22 February 1934, gazetted 17 April 1934.]

13. *Governor may appoint deputy during absence.*-In the event of the Governor having occasion to be temporarily absent for a short period from the seat of Government or from the State, he may, in every such case, by an instrument under the public seal of the State, constitute and appoint our Lieutenant-Governor, or, if there be no such officer or if such officer be absent or unable to act, then any other person, to be his deputy during such temporary absence, and in that capacity to exercise, perform, and execute, for and on behalf of the Governor during such absence, but no longer, all such powers and authorities vested in the Governor by these our letters patent or otherwise as shall in and by such instrument be specified and limited, but no others. Provided, nevertheless, that, by the appointment of a deputy as aforesaid, the power and authority of the Governor shall not be abridged, altered, or in any way affected otherwise than we may at any time hereafter think proper to direct. Provided, further, that the Governor, during his passage to or from the dependencies of the State shall not be deemed to be absent from the State.

[This clause was substituted for previous clause 13 by letters patent of 13 August 1920, gazetted 16 November 1920.]

14. *Officers and others to obey and assist Governor.*-And we do hereby require and command all our officers and Ministers, and all other inhabitants of the State, to be obedient, aiding, and assisting unto the Governor, or to such person or persons as may from time to time, under the provisions of these our letters patent, administer the Government of the State.

15. *Power reserved to Her Majesty to revoke, alter, or amend the present letters patent.*-And we do hereby reserve to ourselves, our heirs and successors, full power and authority from time to time to revoke, alter or amend these our letters patent as to us or them shall seem meet.

16. *Publication of letters patent.*-And we do direct and enjoin that these our letters patent shall be read and proclaimed at such place or places within our said State as the Governor shall think fit.

ROYAL INSTRUCTIONS TO THE GOVERNOR

(This form is taken from the Instructions of 1925 to the Governor of Queensland. The Instructions are substantially the same in the other States.)

I. In these Our Instructions, unless inconsistent with the context, the term "the Governor" shall include every person for the time being administering the Government of the State.

II. The Governor may, whenever he thinks fit, require any person in the public service to take the Oath of Allegiance, together with such other Oath or Oaths as may from time to time be prescribed by any Law in force in the State. The Governor is to administer such Oaths or cause them to be administered by some Public Officer of the State.

III. The Governor shall forthwith communicate these Our Instructions to the Executive Council, and likewise all such others, from time to time, as he shall find convenient for Our service to impart to them.

IV. The Governor shall attend and preside at the meetings of the Executive Council, unless prevented by some necessary or reasonable cause, and in his absence such member as may be appointed by him in that behalf or in the absence of such member the senior member of the Executive Council actually present shall preside; the seniority of the members of the said Council being regulated according to the order of their respective appointments as members thereof.

V. The Executive Council shall not proceed to the despatch of business unless duly summoned by authority of the Governor nor unless two members at least (exclusive of the Governor or of the member presiding) be present and assisting throughout the whole of the meetings at which any such business shall be despatched.

VI. In the execution of the powers and authorities vested in him the Governor shall be guided by the advice of the Executive Council, but if in any case he shall see sufficient cause to dissent from the opinion of the said Council he may act in the exercise of his said powers and authorities in opposition to the opinion of the Council, reporting the matter to Us without delay, with the reasons for his so acting.

In any such case it shall be competent to any member of the said Council to require that there be recorded upon the Minutes of the Council the grounds of any advice or opinion that he may give upon the question.

VII. The Governor shall not, except in the cases hereunder mentioned, assent in Our name to any Bill of any of the following classes:-

1. Any Bill for the divorce of persons joined together in holy matrimony.

2. Any Bill whereby any grant of land or money, or other donation or gratuity, may be made to himself.

3. Any Bill affecting the currency of the State.

4. Any Bill the provision of which shall appear inconsistent with obligations imposed upon Us by Treaty.

5. Any Bill of an extraordinary nature and importance, whereby Our prerogative or the rights and property of Our subjects not residing in the State, or the trade and shipping of the United Kingdom and its Dependencies, may be prejudiced.

6. Any Bill containing provisions to which Our Assent as been once refused, or which have been disallowed by Us;

Unless he shall have previously obtained Our Instructions upon such Bill through one of Our Principal Secretaries of State, or unless such Bill shall contain a clause suspending the operation of such Bill until the signification in the State of Our pleasure thereupon, or unless the Governor shall have satisfied himself that an urgent necessity exists requiring that such Bill be brought into immediate operation, in which case he is authorised to assent in Our name to such Bill, unless the same shall be repugnant to the law of England, or inconsistent with any obligations imposed upon Us by Treaty. But he is to transmit to Us by the earliest opportunity the Bill so assented to, together with his reasons for assenting thereto.

VIII. The Governor shall not pardon or reprieve any offender without first receiving in capital cases the advice of the Executive Council, and in other cases the advice of one, at least, of his Ministers; and in any case in which such pardon or reprieve might directly affect the interests of Our Empire, or of any country or place beyond the jurisdiction of the Government of the State, the Governor shall, before deciding as to either pardon or reprieve, take those interests specially into his own personal consideration in conjunction with such advice as aforesaid.

IX. All Commissions granted by the Governor to any persons to be Judges, Justices of the Peace, or other officers, shall, unless otherwise provided by law, be granted during pleasure only.

X. The Governor shall not quit the State without having first obtained leave from Us for so doing under Our Sign Manual and Signet, or through one of Our Principal Secretaries of State, except for the purpose of visiting the Governor of any neighbouring State or the Governor-General for periods not exceeding one month at any one time, nor exceeding in the aggregate one month for every year's service in the State.

XI. The temporary absence of the Governor for any period not exceeding one month shall not, if he have previously informed the Executive Council, in writing, of his intended absence, and if he have duly appointed a Deputy in accordance with Our said Letters Patent, be deemed a departure from the State within the meaning of the said Letters Patent.

Index